Wil

Blue Ridge Parkway

Wildflowers of the
Blue Ridge Parkway
A Pocket Field Guide

Ann and Rob Simpson

GUILFORD, CONNECTICUT

FALCONGUIDES®

An imprint of Globe Pequot
Falcon and FalconGuides are registered trademarks and Make Adventure
Your Story is a trademark of Rowman & Littlefield.

Distributed by NATIONAL BOOK NETWORK

Copyright © 2017 by Rowman & Littlefield

All interior photographs by Ann and Rob Simpson, unless otherwise
noted.

Maps: Melissa Baker © Rowman & Littlefield

British Library Cataloguing-in-Publication Information available

Library of Congress Cataloging in Publication data available

ISBN 978-0-7627-7011-3 (paperback)
ISBN 978-1-4930-2396-7 (e-book)

♾™ The paper used in this publication meets the minimum
requirements of American National Standard for Information
Sciences—Permanence of Paper for Printed Library Materials, ANSI/NISO
Z39.48-1992.

Contents

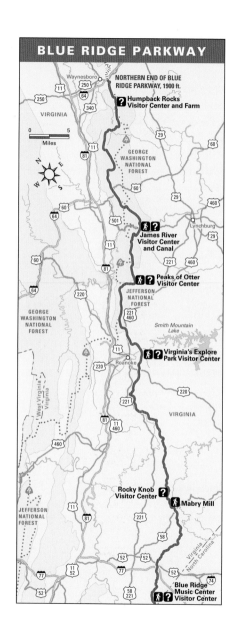

BLUE RIDGE PARKWAY

Waynesboro

NORTHERN END OF BLUE
RIDGE PARKWAY, 1900 ft.

Humpback Rocks
Visitor Center and Farm

VIRGINIA

0   5
Miles

GEORGE
WASHINGTON
NATIONAL
FOREST

Lynchburg

James River
Visitor Center
and Canal

Peaks of Otter
Visitor Center

JEFFERSON
NATIONAL
FOREST

GEORGE
WASHINGTON
NATIONAL
FOREST

Smith Mountain
Lake

Virginia's Explore
Park Visitor Center

Roanoke

West Virginia
Virginia

VIRGINIA

JEFFERSON
NATIONAL
FOREST

Rocky Knob
Visitor Center

Mabry Mill

Virginia
North Carolina

Blue Ridge
Music Center
Visitor Center

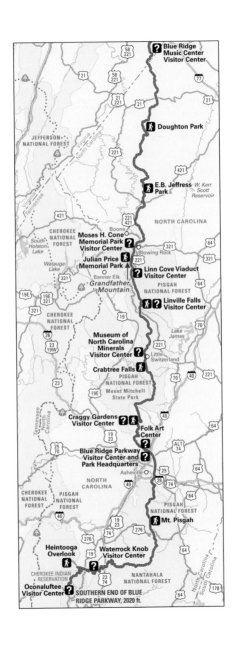

Acknowledgments

Many thanks to the superb park personnel and volunteers of the Blue Ridge Parkway who have dedicated their lives to preserving the natural resources of the park and sharing the natural wonders of the Parkway with visitors. We would especially like to thank Bambi Teague, Chris Ulrey, Aubrey Neas, and Susan Gonshor for sharing their wealth of knowledge about the Blue Ridge Parkway and its natural history. Special thanks go to Karen Searle of Eastern National for her support and encouragement of this project. Our thanks also to Dr. Susan Mills and the staff and members of the Friends of Blue Ridge Parkway for their continued support of the park's interpretative and educational mission. Our sincere appreciation goes to the naturalists and staff at Grandfather Mountain and Mount Mitchell State Park for their dedication in helping to preserve these unique habitats. We would also like to thank all the staff at FalconPress and Rowman & Littlefield, especially David Legere, whose support and efforts have continued to make this National Park Wildflower Guide series a reality.

We would like to dedicate this book to our family, who has supported us with encouragement and understanding during the research, writing, and photography of this wildflower guide. We especially appreciate grandchildren Georgia, Gracie, Jacob, and Natalie, who have inspired this guide. A moment spent sharing nature with a child is an investment in the future of our world. The more a person learns about nature the more he or she begins to realize that this is something worth protecting.

To the reader, this small book is not intended as a complete botanical tome. Keeping botanical terms to a minimum, we have selected some of the most common and interesting wildflowers on and near the Blue Ridge Parkway. We hope this guide helps to open your eyes to the wonders of nature and in doing so will generate a spark of love for the plants and wildflowers that rely on us for their continued existence in important natural habitats such as

the Blue Ridge Parkway. For further information on more wildlife and plants such as trees and shrubs, consult the authors' *Nature Guide to the Blue Ridge Parkway* (Falcon Guides).

Shared Responsibility

The protection of the Blue Ridge Parkway and surrounding region is an immense task, with much at stake. Decades of eroding budgets have reduced staffing and made it more and more difficult to maintain the Parkway's aging and considerable infrastructure to monitor and preserve its many natural and cultural resources and provide education services for visitors. The trend is undeniably clear: Fewer staff members must confront a mountain of threats and try to carry out a dual mission of preserving the Parkway and serving the visiting public. They cannot do it alone. Their success will depend on mobilizing an army of concerned citizens. The Parkway of tomorrow will be defined by the extent to which people today are willing to speak out on behalf of the Parkway and to invest in its future. Fortunately, many nonprofit partner groups now work hand in hand with the Parkway staff. While these organizations have differing missions, they share an overarching goal: to preserve and enhance the national treasure that is the Blue Ridge Parkway.

From early spring through late fall, wildflowers delight the observant in the Southern Appalachians.

Blue Ridge Parkway Association: Promotes travel along the Parkway and provides print and electronic information to visitors about adjacent accommodations, attractions, and communities. blueridgeparkway.org

Blue Ridge Parkway Foundation: Raises funds to support many Parkway programs and projects. brpfoundation.org

Friends of the Blue Ridge Parkway: Promotes volunteerism and leads tree plantings to screen adjacent development. blue ridgefriends.org

Blue Ridge National Heritage Area: Helps operate the Blue Ridge Parkway Visitor Center (Milepost 384) and promotes the preservation and enjoyment of western North Carolina's cultural and natural heritage. blueridgeheritage.com

Eastern National: All you need to do is shop at the nonprofit stores in Parkway visitor centers to enjoy your visit more, support visitor center staffing, and generate cash donations to the Parkway! easternnational.org

Carolina Mountain Club: Provides trail maintenance at the Parkway's southern terminus. carolinamountainclub.org

Conservation Trust for North Carolina (ctnc.org) and the **Blue Ridge Land Conservancy** (blueridgelandconservancy.org): Provide funds to preserve key tracts of land along the Parkway and seek private landowner support.

Blue Ridge Parkway: The Basics

History and Facts

Established: June 30, 1936

Visitors: About 15 million annually; ranks number one in visitation rates in the National Park System

Designations: National Scenic Byway, All-American Road

Natural Heritage Areas: 47

States: Virginia and North Carolina

Time zone: Eastern Standard Time (EST)

Official website: nps.gov/blri

Physical Features

Acreage: 82,439 and 2,776 scenic easements

Elevation: Lowest point: 649.4 feet at James River in Virginia; highest point: 6,047 feet at Richland Balsam in North Carolina; peaks above 5,000 feet: 16

Mountain ranges: 5 in the Central and Southern Appalachians: Blue Ridge, Black, Pisgah, Balsam, Plott Balsam

National forests crossed: 4: George Washington, Jefferson, Nantahala, Pisgah

Miles of boundary: 1,200

Adjacent private landowners: > 4,000; 101 private road accesses

Water resources: 13 lakes; 3 major rivers: James, Roanoke, French Broad; 600 miles of streams; 115 headwaters; 15 watersheds

Average annual precipitation: Ranges from 41.4 inches at Roanoke, Virginia, to 48.1 inches at Asheville, North Carolina

Temperature range (°F): Ranges from -17°F in Asheville, North Carolina, to 105°F in Roanoke, Virginia

Plant species: 2,074 species of vascular plants, including species of wildflowers, trees and shrubs, grasses, sedges, ferns, and fern allies

Plant communities: 75: 32 considered globally rare and 7 of these considered globally imperiled

Animal species: About 320 birds; 72 mammals; 101 fish; 41 reptiles; 58 amphibians; unknown invertebrates

Rare species: 74 globally rare (G1–G3); 9 federally threatened and endangered species; 14 species of concern

Facilities

Entrances: Begin at Milepost 0 at the south end of Shenandoah National Park in Waynesboro, Virginia; end at Milepost 469 at the eastern entrance to Great Smoky Mountains National Park in Cherokee, North Carolina

Visitor centers: 14: Humpback Rocks at Milepost 5.8; James River at Milepost 63.6; Peaks of Otter at Milepost 85.6; Virginia's Explore Park at Milepost 115.1; Rocky Knob at Milepost 169; Blue Ridge Music Center at Milepost 213; Moses Cone Park at Milepost 294; Linn Cove Viaduct at Milepost 304.4; Linville Falls at Milepost 316.4; Museum of North Carolina Minerals at Milepost 330.9; Craggy Gardens at Milepost 364.6; Folk Art Center at Milepost 382.2; Blue Ridge Parkway Visitor Center at Milepost 384 ; Waterrock Knob at Milepost 451.2

Roads: 558 miles; 469 miles of scenic road

State secondary road accesses: 199: 104 in Virginia, 95 in North Carolina

Tunnels: 26; 1 in Virginia, 25 in North Carolina

Overlooks: 382; 281 scenic overlooks, 101 parking areas

Roadside vistas: 910 maintained

Views: 1,228

Trails: 369 miles of trails, including portions of the Appalachian National Scenic Trail and Mountains-to-Sea Trail

The Parkway provides protected habitat for Southern Appalachian endemic plants such as Gray's lily.

Campgrounds: 8 (942 sites): Otter Creek at Milepost 60.9; Peaks of Otter at Milepost 86.0; Rocky Knob at Milepost 167.1; Doughton Park at Milepost 239.2; Julian Price Memorial Park at Milepost 297.0; Linville Falls at Milepost 316.3; Crabtree Falls at Milepost 339.5; Mount Pisgah at Milepost 408.6.

Picnic areas: 15: Humpback Rocks at Milepost 8.5; James River at Milepost 63.6; Peaks of Otter at Milepost 85.6; Roanoke Mountain at Milepost 120.4; Smart View at Milepost 154.5; Rocky Knob at Milepost 169; Groundhog Mountain at Milepost 188.8; Cumberland Knob at Milepost 217.5; Doughton Park at Milepost 241.1; E. B. Jeffress Park at Milepost 271.9; Julian Price Memorial Park at Milepost 296.4; Linville Falls at Milepost 316.4; Crabtree Falls at Milepost 340.2; Craggy Gardens at Milepost 367.6; Mount Pisgah at Milepost 407.8. Many Parkway overlooks also have picnic tables.

Lodging: 2: Peaks of Otter at Milepost 85.6; Pisgah Inn at Milepost 408.8. Check park website for current availability of other lodging at nps.gov/blri/planyourvisit/lodging.htm.

Food: Peaks of Otter at Milepost 85.6; Mabry Mill at Milepost 176.2; Northwest Trading Post at Milepost 258.7; Pisgah Inn & Restaurant at Milepost 408.8. Check park website for current availability of dining at nps.gov/blri/planyourvisit/eatingsleeping.htm.

Fuel: Gasoline is not available on the Parkway but is available in many nearby towns.

Introduction

From high atop overlooks on the Blue Ridge Parkway, an ocean of mountains roll endlessly in a blue haze of hollows and swells as far as you can see. Creatively designed as a scenic drive for motorists, the Parkway is a unique way to see the Blue Ridge Mountains. Stretching for 469 miles atop the ancient Appalachian Mountains, the roadway passes through one of the most biologically diverse habitats in the world, with more than 10,000 documented species of organisms. The cool high-elevation forest habitats that are normally found in more northern climates allow many species of plants to survive here, such as red spruce (*Picea rubens*), northern wild raisin (*Viburnum nudum*), painted trillium (*Trillium undulatum*), bluebead lily (*Clintonia borealis*), and yellow nodding ladies' tresses (*Spiranthes ochroleuca*).

Looking across the rolling mountains, it is difficult to imagine that millions of years ago these gentle peaks were as tall as the relatively newly formed Rocky Mountains of the West. Untouched by glaciers that once covered the land to the north, the Southern Appalachians are one of the most biologically diverse areas in the

A blended family of native and nonnative wildflowers call the Blue Ridge Parkway home.

world. The floral diversity of the Appalachians ranges from plants that grow at low elevations along rivers to the hardiest plants that can withstand the cold high elevations above 6,000 feet. With the exception of the rain forests of Central and South America, Appalachian flora is unsurpassed in the world.

Wildflowers of Blue Ridge Parkway is an easy-to-use pocket-size field guide to help visitors identify some of the most common wildflowers and selected flowering shrubs of the park. Technical terms have been kept to a minimum, and color pictures accompany the descriptions. Perfectly sized to fit easily into a daypack, this compact field guide is packed with interesting information about each plant, including natural history notes, ethnobotanical information, and other historical remarks. We care for the things we know. Intended as an introduction to the wildflowers of the park, this small book will hopefully spark an interest in the natural world and generate further interest in the care for and support of the environment. Refer to the "Selected References" section at the end of this book for further information and sources for in-depth identification. For further infor-

A dizzying array of wildflowers awaits visitors throughout the blooming seasons.

mation on the Parkway's native plants, contact the Virginia Native Plant Society (vnps.org) and North Carolina Native Plant Society (ncwildflower.org).

About the Blue Ridge Parkway

The Blue Ridge Parkway beckons visitors from around the world to its magnificent vistas, crashing waterfalls, cool mountain streams, and wildflower-filled meadows. Designated as a National

Scenic Byway and an All-American Road in 2005, the Parkway ranks number one in visitation in the National Park System, with about 15 million visitors annually. Planned as a slow-paced "drive for a while, stop for a while" recreational road, the Parkway allows motorists to cruise along at an easy 45 miles per hour, enjoying the journey on a road that is longer than mainland Florida. The Parkway passes through some of the most magnificent mountain scenery on the East Coast, traversing five mountain ranges and four national forests as it passes through both Virginia and North Carolina on its ramble between Shenandoah and Great Smoky Mountains National Parks.

We highly recommend that you begin your visit with a stop at one of the fourteen visitor centers, where you can pick up a Parkway map and learn about activities such as the Junior Rangers and other programs. Along the roadway you will notice numbered mileposts that begin with 0 at Rockfish Gap near Waynesboro, Virginia, and end at 469 near Cherokee, North Carolina. There is no entrance fee to the Blue Ridge Parkway. Although the Parkway is open year-round, most visitor services are only open from mid-May to late October/early November. Some sections of the Parkway itself may be temporarily closed in winter. You can check road closures by calling the park information line (828-298-0398) or on the park website (nps.gov/blri). At a maximum speed limit of 45 miles per hour, theoretically you could drive the 469 miles in about 11 hours, but due to the mountainous terrain, slow-moving vehicles, construction, wildlife, and safety concerns, you should allow about 30 miles per hour when figuring your actual travel time.

Optimally you should allow at least four days of leisurely travel time to enjoy the scenic beauty of this exquisite land. The journey requires careful planning, as there is no fuel available on the Parkway and limited food and lodging. Most visitors make food stops and lodging reservations at the local towns bordering the Parkway. See "Mileposts of Common Destinations on or near the Parkway" for help with planning your visit. The Blue Ridge Parkway Association publishes a helpful online directory for assistance with trip planning and gas station locations (blueridge parkway.org). There are twenty-five Parkway tunnels in North Carolina and one in Virginia, some of which may limit the ability of large motor homes to pass. Check the park website (nps.gov/ blri/planyourvisit/tunnel-heights.htm) for more information as you plan your trip.

The Parkway comes to life in April and May, when the first brave wildflowers stretch through the blanket of fallen brown leaves to bask in the warming sun. Mid-June brings gorgeous mountain laurel and rhododendron blooms that cover the roadway and trails in a canopy of pink flowers.

In autumn the surrounding communities share their stories with leaf peepers who have come to the mountains to savor the glorious fall show. Taking great pictures is easy along the Parkway, with photographers finding enchanting subjects at every turn. Hundreds of trails are available—from easy leg-stretchers for time-pressed visitors to the Mountains-to-Sea and Appalachian Trails, which challenge marathon hikers. Waterfalls are on the "must see" list for many park visitors; fortunately there are many to choose from, including Crabtree, Linville, and the falls at Graveyard Fields.

Mileposts of Common Destinations on or near the Parkway

Most visitor services on the Parkway are open mid-May through late October or early November. Camping reservations for most campgrounds on the Parkway may be made at recreation.gov, or call (877) 444-6777. All others are on a first-come, first-served basis. There is no fuel available on the Parkway, but fuel and other services may be found at many towns just off the Parkway. Note that there may be lengthy distances between fuel stops; plan accordingly.

Note: In the following section, **MP** = milepost on the Blue Ridge Parkway. Bold print denotes destinations on the Parkway. Restrooms are located at visitor centers and at most picnic areas.

MP	VIRGINIA
0.0	**Rockfish Gap**—north entrance to Blue Ridge Parkway
	Waynesboro—4 miles west on US 250; lodging, food, fuel
	Shenandoah National Park south entrance; nps.gov/shen
5.8	**Humpback Rocks**—visitor center, picnic area, hiking, 1890s era Mountain Farm
13.5	Wintergreen Resort—1 mile east on VA 664; lodging, food, fuel, nature center, fishing, hiking; the Nature Foundation at Wintergreen; VA 664, Wintergreen, VA; (434) 325-2200; wintergreenresort.com
16.0	Sherando Lake Recreation Area, VA 814; George Washington National Forest, campground, swimming, boating, fishing
45.6	Buena Vista—5 miles west on US 60; lodging, food, fuel
	Lexington—11 miles west on US 60; lodging, food, fuel
60.9	**Otter Creek**—campground, fishing, hiking
61.6	Natural Bridge—15 miles west on US 501; National Historic Landmark; lodging, food, fuel, hiking; 15 Appledore Lane, Natural Bridge, VA; (800) 533-1410; naturalbridgeva.com
63.6	Lynchburg—22 miles east on US 501; lodging food, fuel
63.8	**James River**—visitor center, picnic, fishing, hiking, restored canal locks, Trail of Trees
83.5	**Fallingwater Cascades**—hiking, waterfall
86.0	**Peaks of Otter**—visitor center, exhibits, nature center, lodging, food, picnic, campground, gift store, fishing, hiking, 1930s era historic Johnson Farm
	Peaks of Otter Lodge, 85554 Blue Ridge Pkwy., Bedford, VA; reservations (866) 387-9905, front desk (540) 586-1081; peaksofotter.com
115.1	Virginia's Explore Park—visitor information center, hiking, mountain biking trails, historical buildings, gift shop, river access; (540) 427-1800 or (540) 387-6078; explorepark.org
120.4	Roanoke—lodging, food, fuel, hospital, all services; 105.8 US 460, 112.2 VA 24; 120.4 Mill Mountain Spur Road, 121.4 US 220
	Roanoke Mountain Picnic Area—picnic, hiking
	Mill Mountain Park Discovery Center and Zoo; hiking, wildflower garden, Roanoke Star, Discovery Center, picnic area; (540) 853-1236; playroanoke.com/parks-and-greenways/mill-mountain-park-2; mmzoo.org
154.4	**Smart View**—picnic, hiking

297.1 **Julian Price Memorial Park**—campground, picnic, hiking, fishing, canoe/boat rentals

304.4 **Linn Cove Viaduct**—visitor center, hiking, award-winning engineering design

305.1 Linville—3 miles on US 221; lodging, food, fuel

Grandfather Mountain—1 mile from Parkway (Linville exit) to US 221; International Biosphere Reserve, mile-high swinging bridge, wildlife and nature exhibits, native plant garden, 16 natural communities with 70 rare or endangered species, 29 of which are globally imperiled; 2050 Blowing Rock Hwy., Linville, NC; (800) 468-7325; grandfather.com

Sugar Mountain—8 miles on US 221, south to NC 184 North; lodging, food, fuel, hiking, skiing; sugarmountain.northcarolina.com

305.2 Banner Elk—10 miles north on NC 184/194; lodging, food, fuel

308.2 **Flat Rock Parking Area**—hiking, self-guiding nature trail

316.4 **Linville Falls**—visitor center, Linville Falls waterfall, campground, picnic, hiking, fishing

328.3 **Orchard at Altapass**—gifts, food, apple orchards, Monarch Butterfly Conservation Center and butterfly gardens, Appalachian culture display; 1025 Orchard Rd., Spruce Pine, NC; (828) 765-9531; altapassorchard.com

331.0 **Museum of North Carolina Minerals**—visitor center

Spruce Pine—6 miles north on NC 226; lodging, food, fuel

334.0 Little Switzerland—NC 226A just off Parkway; lodging, food, fuel

339.5 **Crabtree Falls**—campground, hiking, Crabtree Falls waterfall

355.4 **Mount Mitchell State Park**—via NC 128; highest point east of the Mississippi River; observation tower, natural history museum, gifts, camping, food, hiking; 2388 NC 128, Burnsville, NC; (828) 675-4611; ncparks.gov/mount-mitchell -state-park

364.5 **Craggy Gardens Visitor Center**—visitor center, hiking

367.6 **Craggy Gardens**—picnic area, hiking

376.6 Ox Creek Road—Rattlesnake Lodge Hiking Trail, NC 694, Elk Mountain Scenic Highway, 8 miles to Weaverville

382.0 **Folk Art Center**—National Park Information Center, Southern Highland Craft Guild; gifts, crafts, craft demonstrations, Appalachian culture display; (828) 298-7928; southernhighlandguild.org/folk-art-center

April and May launch the pageant of spring, such as trails of charming trillium.

Safety Notes

The driving experience on the Blue Ridge Parkway is uniquely designed to afford motorists with spectacular views that follow the natural flow of the mountains. The Parkway speed limit is generally 45 miles per hour, but in some areas it drops to 25 miles per hour or less. In the Roanoke, Virginia, and Asheville, North Carolina, areas, the speed limit is 35 miles per hour. There are some steep grades and many winding curves, some with very little sight distances. There are tight spiral curves in some places and areas with narrow shoulders—motorists should slow down in these areas. When passing through one of the twenty-six tunnels on the Parkway, turn on your headlights and watch for cyclists in the tunnel. The Parkway is a favorite destination drive for bicyclists and motorcyclists. Be sure to watch out for them and give them plenty of space. Perhaps the greatest distractions are the magnificent views. Allow time to pull over and enjoy the scenery, and be aware that others may be distracted by the view and not paying attention to the road. Also be aware that wildlife such as bears and deer may dash onto the road with little notice. Fog often envelops the roadway, especially at the higher elevations—slow down in foggy conditions. When it is snowy or icy, avoid the Parkway altogether.

Always let someone know when you go for a hike. Dress in layers, and carry rain gear and plenty of water; weather conditions can change rapidly. Be aware of fast-moving streams and waterfalls. Falling trees and branches can present hazards. Dehydration and sunburn can be prevented by drinking plenty of water and applying sunscreen to all exposed areas. Do not drink untreated water from springs or streams—the seemingly clean water may harbor parasites such as *Giardia lamblia*, which causes severe diarrhea.

Never feed wildlife. It is not only illegal but also endangers the welfare of the animal. Stay a safe distance from all wildlife. There are venomous snakes (timber rattlesnakes and copperheads) along the Parkway; be careful where you place your hands and feet, especially when climbing on rocks or in shrubby areas. Although there are no grizzly bears here, black bears do reside in the park. Most will avoid you if they hear you coming. Avoid hiking alone, and never let small children run ahead of you on trails. Keep them beside you, and pick them up immediately if you encounter a bear. Ticks and mosquitoes are common throughout the park; take precautions, such as applying insect repellent and tucking your pants into your socks to prevent bites that may result in Lyme disease or Rocky Mountain spotted fever.

Report emergencies such as accidents, uncontrolled fires, or other safety hazards by calling (800) PARK-WATCH (800-727-5928) or 911.

Conservation Note

Please leave wildflowers and other plants where they grow. When hiking, stay on established trails and watch where you put your feet to avoid damaging plants. Especially in cliff areas, avoid trampling plants—some of them may only be able to exist in these special conditions.

Along the Blue Ridge Parkway, limited quantities of berries, fruits, and nuts may be gathered for personal consumption.

Digging, picking, or damaging plants in a national park is a federal offense and can result in fines and/or a prison sentence. Plant poachers illegally harvest certain plant species in these federally protected lands. Make sure to alert a park official if you suspect harvesting of any plants along the Parkway. For more information on the park and ways you can help, visit nps.gov/blri.

Nonnative Plants

Many flowers and trees along the Parkway were planted here by families wishing to bring familiar plants from their homelands. Some plants arrived here as seeds stuck to clothing or animal fur. Some of these nonnative plants are invasive and thrive in this rich habitat, choking out native plants that have historically grown in the forests and meadows. Parkway botanists have identified ten of these plants as the "least wanted plants along the Blue Ridge Parkway" and are working to keep them from destroying native plants.

- Tree of heaven (*Ailanthus altissima*)
- Princess tree (*Paulownia tomentosa*)
- Oriental bittersweet (*Celastrus orbiculatus*)
- Japanese spirea (*Spiraea japonica*)
- Multiflora rose (*Rosa multiflora*)
- Coltsfoot (*Tussilago farfara*)
- Japanese stiltgrass (*Microstegium vimineum*)
- Garlic mustard (*Alliaria petiolata*)
- Air potato (*Dioscorea bulbifera*)
- Chinese silver grass (*Miscanthus sinensis*)

How to Use This Guide

In an effort to create consistent communication worldwide, each plant has a Latin name—genus and species—that is unique to that plant. Common names of families are given with the scientific family name in parentheses. In many cases, an organism may have many common names, often varying by locality. In addition, genetic research is rapidly discovering new inherent relationships and associations; therefore the taxonomic status of many organisms may change with the new information. In general, plants are listed by color then alphabetically by family and then genus. The taxonomic designations used follow those listed in the *Flora of the Southern and Mid-Atlantic States*, the working draft of May 21, 2015, by Alan S. Weakley from the University of North Carolina.

Photo Tips

Sharp focus is the key to taking great nature photos. Overcast days offer nice soft lighting for wildflowers. In deep shade, increase the ISO or use a flash. Bright sunny days create harsh shadows, and a flash is needed to add detail to the dark shaded areas of the flower. Image stabilization capability on the lens will help stop camera motion. For more advanced camera systems, shooting close-ups at f16 with a flash will give more depth of field and stop motion from wind. When taking wildflower photos, be careful not to trample other plants. A tripod is necessary for low lighting conditions in the early morning or evening.

Staying in touch with nature, learning her secrets, and exploring her intricacies deepens your understanding of the wonder of life.

Suggested Wildflower Areas and Hikes near the Blue Ridge Parkway

The following areas or trails are suggested for the general public and families who want to see wildflowers along the Blue Ridge Parkway. The milepost (MP) is given from north to south along the Parkway. Some of the recommended areas and trails are wheelchair accessible or accessible with assistance. It is a good idea to first stop at a visitor center and check with a park ranger to find out what is currently blooming in the area. To find other attractive hikes, consult a topographic map or hiking guides such as Randy Johnson's *Best Easy Day Hikes* and *Hiking the Blue Ridge Parkway* (FalconGuides). These and other interpretive publications are offered in Parkway visitor centers. Please do not pick any wildflowers or remove any natural objects from the park.

With such a long, narrow park, it is most convenient to refer to four sections subdivided loosely by physiographic regions from north to south for 469 miles. See "Mileposts of Common Destinations on or near the Parkway" for further information.

Ridge District (Mileposts 0–106)

- **Humpback Rocks—MP 5.8.** The short Mountain Farm Trail leads past several typical Appalachian homestead buildings where volunteers may demonstrate handicrafts and typical music. In the wetland areas near the visitor center, watch for the yellow flowers of green and gold blooming near the forest edges. In fall, turtlehead and cardinal flower add interesting color to the wetland.

- **Greenstone Self-Guiding Trail—MP 8.8.** A nice leg-stretcher on a 0.2-mile forested loop with a few rocky areas leads to a view into the Shenandoah Valley. Here watch for stonecrop, Solomon's seal, southern harebell, and bouncing Bet. White snakeroot and goldenrods line the trail in fall.

- **James River—MP 63.8.** At 649.4 feet above sea level, the James River area is the lowest elevation on the Parkway. The riparian (river's edge) habitat provides moisture for plants such as Virginia bluebells. The self-guiding 0.5-mile Trail of Trees is a great place to learn to identify native Southern Appalachian hardwoods; many of the trees along the trail are labeled with their name and natural history information. Along this trail look for yucca, false Solomon's seal, and beechdrops.

- **Peaks of Otter—MP 86.** Abbott Lake Loop is an easy 1-mile trail around peaceful Abbott Lake, whose smooth waters reflect pyramid-shaped Sharp Top Mountain. In May look for a special fluted species of jack-in-the-pulpit with deep ridges in the spade that may be blooming in wet areas amid the large leaves of skunk cabbage. Quite a few species of violets line the trail in spring. The lavender flowers of beebalm are some of the first summer flowers to bloom here. Late summer and fall bring spotted jewelweed in the wet areas plus cheery crownbeard in the dry meadows.

Plateau District (Mileposts 107–217)

- **Roanoke Area—MPs 115–120.4.** The Roanoke area is typically one of the drier portions of the Parkway. In this habitat look for such flowers as bird's-foot violet, as well as moss phlox growing under pitch and mountain pines. Just off the Parkway, Virginia's Explore Park offers easy trails through a wooded area, and the Mill Mountain Zoo and Discovery Center boasts a wonderful wildflower garden with handy labels lovingly cared for by the local garden club.
- **Rakes Mill Pond—MP 162.4.** An easy walk along the pond affords you a look at some interesting wetland wildflowers such as monkeyflower, spotted touch-me-not, and tall rue.
- **Mabry Mill—MP 176.2.** The iconic Mabry Mill is undoubtedly the most photographed place on the Parkway. It is also a great place to see a good selection of flora and fauna. A fantastic display of southern red trillium graces the accessible trail in April and May. In late May and early June, Catawba rhododendrons provide photographers a colorful addition to their pictures of the mill and pond. Other wildflowers that bloom throughout the season include violets, saxifrage, skunk cabbage, mayapple, and Carolina bugbane.
- **Blue Ridge Music Center—MP 213.** Humming along with the strum of banjos and the singing of fiddles, your visit to the Blue Ridge Music Center wouldn't be complete without a hike on the High Meadow Trail or Fisher Peak Loop trail. Walking even a short distance on the Fisher Peak Loop, lined

in season with the pink blossoms of mountain laurel, you can spy a large number of interesting wildflowers. Look for an abundance of spring violets along the trail and specialties such as nodding ladies' tresses. The wetland at the beginning of the trail is filled with irises, sneezeweed, cardinal flower, and ironweed. In the open meadow, butterflies sip nectar from milkweeds and asters.

Highlands District (Mileposts 218–305)

- **Doughton Park—MP 241.1.** Near Laurel Springs, North Carolina, Doughton Park is a quiet area of the Parkway filled with rolling meadows that speak of a time when the days were simple and reflective. The prairie-like area is filled with wildflowers including dense blazing star, butterfly milkweed, coreopsis, and thistles—all of which attract myriad butterflies. Bring a picnic lunch and enjoy the peaceful hum of bees busy at work in the abundant meadows.
- **E. B. Jeffress Park—MP 272.** The Cascades Trail never disappoints as the seasons proceed from early spring ephemerals such as bloodroot and cut-leaf toothwort to summer plants including pinesap. Mountain laurel and great rhododendron usher hikers along the trail to the overlook at the cascades of Falls Creek. Fall finds the trail lined with goldenrods and asters that peek out from abundant mushrooms growing beneath the shading shrubbery.
- **Moses Cone Park—MP 294.1.** Mountain laurel and Catawba rhododendron line the trails and carriage roads at Moses Cone Park near the Flat Top manor house. In nearby Boone you can stroll through the wildflowers in the Daniel Boone Native Gardens. Acid-loving wildflowers such as trailing arbutus can be found under the tall heath shrubs.
- **Julian Price Memorial Park—MPs 295.1–298.0.** This is a great place to spot painted trillium if you are visiting in the springtime. The 2.4-mile hike around Price Lake is easy, and parts are on a boardwalk over wet areas. Another common

flower here is false lily of the valley. In spring look for creamy white mayapple flowers that nod beneath the large maple-like leaves in rich woods. Tall goldenrod puts on a bright show in autumn.

- **Linn Cove Viaduct—MP 304.4.** A short 0.15-mile paved trail from the Linn Cove Visitor Center parking lot leads to a view under the viaduct where you can see lots of interesting wildflowers, including wild geranium, beebalm, and violets. At 4,315 feet in elevation, the cool mountain air provides moist habitat for special wildflowers such as umbrella leaf, turtlehead, and false hellebore that grow in wet seepage areas. The strenuous Tanawha Trail continues to Rough Ridge, where you can spy the tiny flowers of sand myrtle growing near the boardwalk.

- **Grandfather Mountain—MP 305.1.** Just off the Parkway, Grandfather Mountain is a stop not to be missed. Part North Carolina state park and part nature preserve administered by the Grandfather Mountain Stewardship Foundation (admission fee), Grandfather Mountain protects some of the rarest plants and animals in the Blue Ridge Mountains. The mountain's 5,946-foot summit provides outstanding vistas from the mile-high swinging bridge. The surrounding area hosts such special wildflowers as pine barrens death-camas and sand myrtle. The wildflower garden attracts myriad butterflies, including swallowtails and fritillaries. So special is this place that

Breathtakingly beautiful displays of Catawba rhododendron line the Parkway in May and June.

in 1992 it was named an International Biosphere Reserve. Within its boundaries are sixteen distinct ecological communities that protect seventy-three rare or endangered species of plants and animals including Blue Ridge goldenrod, Heller's blazing star, and Roan Mountain bluet.

Pisgah District (Mileposts 306–469)

- **Flat Rock Trail—MP 308.** In the Pisgah District, the Blue Ridge Parkway passes through the accessible highest points along the drive. The Flat Rock loop is only about a 0.7-mile circuit, but it does involve a bit of a climb up to the flat rock quartzite outcrop with views into Linville Valley. Signs along the way tell the story of forest trees and geology. The trail is decorated with abundant wildflowers, including Solomon's seal and false Solomon's seal, white clintonia, jack-in-the-pulpit, lily of the valley, fly poison, and primrose-leaved violet.
- **Linville Falls—MP 316.4.** A 1.6-mile moderate round-trip hike to see the plunging waters leap over the ancient rock face is one of the most popular Parkway attractions. Along the trail to the falls you can see Carolina rhododendron, wild geranium, wild yam, Indian cucumber root, wild ginger, big-flowered hexastylis, and fringed phacelia.
- **Crabtree Falls—MP 339.5.** A 2.5-mile popular but strenuous loop hike to a waterfall can reward plant lovers with many flowers in their blooming season. In July, rosebay, or great, rhododendrons display their large white blossoms. Flowers such as fire pink, showy orchis, large-flowered trillium, and Dutchman's pipe decorate the woodlands.
- **Mount Mitchell State Park—MP 355.3.** Although not administered by the Blue Ridge Parkway, the Mount Mitchell State Park entrance is directly off the drive on NC 128. At an elevation of 6,684 feet, this is the highest point on the East Coast, and only specialized plants can survive the cold temperatures and harsh winters here. Plants such as white or Appalachian turtlehead can be seen along the 0.3-mile paved

trail to the observation tower. Red spruce forests harbor such wildflowers as Michaux's saxifrage and filmy angelica.

- **Craggy Gardens—MP 364.6.** One of the most common questions asked of park rangers is where the "gardens" at Craggy Gardens are located. Craggy Gardens was so named for the spectacular views and miles of pink-blossomed Catawba rhododendrons, which typically bloom in the second or third week of June, although some years the show is already over by then or may be waiting until later in the month. Mountain meadow rue and Carolina bugbane can be found along the trail to the balds. The Craggy Pinnacle Trail is a 0.6-mile hike to the summit. A 3-mile drive south will bring you to the entrance to the Craggy Gardens picnic area, also decorated in Catawba rhododendrons. In the wooded areas and along the trails, keep an eye out for spring wildflowers such as red trilliums and umbrella leaf.

- **Blue Ridge Parkway Visitor Center—MP 384.** The Blue Ridge Parkway Visitor Center has a lovely garden at the entrance and throughout the parking area, planted with native wildflowers that have convenient nametags. Hiking trails in this area include the Rattlesnake Lodge Trail, along which you may see such unusual plants as pygmy pipes and lettuce-leaf saxifrage. The Asheville area offers several great opportunities to view wildflowers, including the Botanical Gardens at Asheville, the North Carolina Arboretum, and the Western North Carolina Nature Center. The famed Biltmore Estate and gardens also is located near the Blue Ridge Parkway.

- **Mount Pisgah—MP 408.6.** This high-altitude habitat supports a unique and varied population of plants and animals that thrive in the cool temperatures. In the campground there is a bog supporting a variety of interesting plants, including smooth alder, angelica, and mushrooms such as chanterelles. Here eastern chipmunks dart about and feed on the tasty blossoms of leather flower. Pink turtlehead grows here along with the tall yellow flowers of green-headed coneflower. South of Pisgah you can take US 276 South for 4 miles for a highly recommended visit to the Forest Discovery Center, which has interpretative hiking trails and native wildflower gardens.

- **Graveyard Fields—MP 418.8.** Graveyard Fields contains a 3.2-mile partial loop trail in a 5,120-foot-elevation valley, filled with blueberries and flowing streams. The Yellowstone Prong of the Pigeon River flows through the valley. At one time the valley was filled with spruce and fir trees, but effects of a great windstorm, major forest fires, and logging have reduced the trees in the area. Shrubs such as blueberries thrive in the sun-filled open valley, and along the creek's side trails you can find fetterbush, Appalachian bush honeysuckle, trilliums, and St. John's wort. About 4 miles south of Graveyard Fields you can climb the short but steep trail to the summit of Devil's Courthouse. Make sure to stay on the trail here—the fragile plant life can easily be trampled and destroyed.

- **Richland Balsam Trail—MP 431.0.** The trail to the highest accessible point on the Parkway, Richland Balsam, starts at the Haywood-Jackson Overlook, which peers into the Shining Rock Wilderness. The 1.5-mile (round-trip) moderate trail climbs gradually through a cool spruce-fir forest with trees draped in misty lichens. A hiking pole will help you navigate over and around roots in the trail. Trail markers guide the way with information on the flora and fauna. At the 6,410-foot summit, you can catch your breath while enjoying wildflowers such as Blue Ridge white heart-leaved aster, Appalachian white snakeroot, and skunk goldenrod. This point is the tenth-highest peak in the Appalachians.

- **Waterrock Knob—MP 451.2.** Ladies' tresses, goldenrods, yarrow, filmy angelica, and Appalachian white snakeroot are some of the flowers that bloom at this high elevation of 5,820 feet. The strenuous trail to the summit climbs to 6,292 feet. If you don't want to climb all the way to the top, you can bring a picnic lunch and enjoy the spectacular views from the picnic tables adjacent to the parking lot, which is surrounded by a nice display of summer and fall wildflowers.

- **Heintooga Overlook Spur Road—MP 458.2.** A short 3.6-mile jaunt off the Parkway that leads into neighboring Great Smoky Mountains National Park offers quiet overlooks sporting such wildflowers as wavy-leaved and Lowery's asters, featherbells, and great Indian plantain. The tall yellow blooms of green-headed coneflowers attract a large number of butterflies. In mornings and evenings, elk often venture into the open areas to nibble on meadow grasses and tasty clovers.

Ecosystems

Following the Blue Ridge Mountains for 469 miles, the Parkway passes through five mountain ranges in the Central and Southern Appalachians and four national forests. As the longest continuous route into the Appalachian Mountains, the Parkway plays a major role in the protection of some of the most biologically diverse habitats in the United States. With an elevation range along the Parkway from roughly 650 feet at the James River to 6,047 feet at Richland Balsam, the diversity of flora and fauna is exceptional.

Conservation efforts along the Blue Ridge Parkway help protect over 2,000 species of vascular plants that live in the park's more than seventy-five distinct plant communities.

More than 2,074 species of vascular plants have been identified here, including 24 that are considered globally rare and 7 that are globally imperiled.

About 11,000 years ago glaciers covered land as close as Pennsylvania to the north but didn't reach Virginia or North Carolina. Some of the northern species that were forced south still remain in the Blue Ridge on the high, cool mountain peaks. Minute genetic changes in these isolated populations, called relics, eventually result in species diversification.

The forest types of the Blue Ridge range from the drier oak-hickories in the northern section to the lush cove forests of magnolias and tulip trees in the central section. The southern-most section in the high elevations of the Balsam Mountains is characterized by dark green spruce and fir trees. The trees release isoprene, causing the bluish haze that engendered the name Blue Ridge Mountains.

FILMY ANGELICA
Angelica triquinata
Carrot family (Apiaceae)

Quick ID: Tiny green to greenish-white flowers, flower heads 3" to 6" across in a group (umbel) with 15–25 rays on top of tall stem; coarsely toothed, highly divided leaves up to 12" long, leaflets tapering to a long point, stalks of the upper leaves dilated and partially clasping stem; stout green, smooth stem is tinged red; flattened, winged seed capsules in pairs.

Height: 2'–5'   **Bloom Season:** July–September

Filmy angelica is a high-elevation Appalachian endemic often forming large colonies in moist woods or on balds. The greenish flowers are formed into a rounded to flattened head called an umbel. The flowers exude copious sweet nectar that attracts bees, wasps, and hornets, including parasitic yellow jackets (*Dolichovespula arctica*). These and other pollinators that sip at the nectar soon find themselves unable to fly or even walk away without staggering, as the nectar is strongly intoxicating. Other members of this family are extremely toxic, including poison hemlock (*Conium maculatum*), which can cause respiratory failure if eaten. You can see filmy angelica in moist areas at Pisgah Campground, the Cascades Trail at E. B. Jeffress Park, and at balds such as Craggy Gardens and nearby Roan Mountain.

JACK-IN-THE-PULPIT
Arisaema triphyllum
Arum family (Araceae)

Quick ID: 3 oval pointed leaflets atop the stem; spike (spadix) of tiny, insignificant flowers covered by light green hood (spathe) with white or purplish stripes; fruits are clusters of bright red berries on the stalk.

Height: 8"–24"   **Bloom Season:** April–June

Jack-in-the-pulpit can be found in forested habitats in most areas along the Parkway. The tiny flowers are found on a fleshy spike called a spadix (Jack), and a showy bract called a spathe (pulpit) surrounds the spadix. Perhaps the best place to see this plant is in the Peaks of Otter area, where 2 species can be found, including the unusual bog jack-in-the-pulpit (*A. stewardsonii*) (inset). Sporting deeply fluted ridges with green or purple stripes on the hood (spathe), it is typically found in moist sites in northern states and Canada. The underground corms contain crystals of calcium oxalate, which cause a needlelike burning sensation if chewed. Young pranksters dubbed it "memory plant" after tempting unknowing visitors into trying a bite—one they would always remember.

SKUNK CABBAGE
Symplocarpus foetidus
Arum family (Araceae)
Quick ID: Tiny yellow flowers on rounded spike (spadix); mottled green to purple shell-like 3"–6" sheath (spathe); large, broad, veined, dark green leaves to 1' wide and up to 2' long on stalk rising from ground.
Height: 1'–2'   **Bloom Season:** February–April

Camouflaged, blooming in winter, and with an odor of rotting meat, skunk cabbage is a flower that survives against all odds. Unique in the flower world, skunk cabbage is able to generate heat up to 68 toasty degrees, even when the ambient temperature falls below 0°F. This process, called thermogenesis, can melt fallen snow around the plant and allows the flower to bloom in the coldest weather. Competing with winter-killed carcasses, the heady aroma of blooming skunk cabbage is irresistible to flies and other insects that may be active in late winter. Snails and beetles are also attracted to the plant's warmth, seeking refuge within its protective sheath. Look for skunk cabbage in wet, marshy areas such as those at Mabry Mill and near the James River and Otter Creek.

POISON IVY
Toxicodendron radicans
Sumac family (Anacardiaceae)

Quick ID: Tiny bell-shaped greenish-white flowers; 3 leaflets with pointed tips each 2"–4½" long; climbing vine or trailing vine or shrub; small round whitish fruits.

Height: Vine to 150'   **Bloom Season:** April–May

The inconspicuous tiny greenish-white flowers of poison ivy are typically not the first part of this infamous plant that people notice. Poison ivy can appear as a trailing vine 4"–10" tall or as a shrub up to 4'. It may also form a climbing vine resembling a fuzzy rope that grows up to 150' on trees. Poison ivy contains urushiol, an oil that causes a skin reaction in 80 percent of people. Folk remedies such as pouring bleach on the rash, eating the leaves, or rubbing the leaves on the rash may cause more harm. Wash the affected area with cool water and soap, and remember the saying "Leaves of three, let it be."

WILD GINGER
Asarum canadense
Birthwort family (Aristolochiaceae)
Quick ID: Maroon-brown, urn-shaped flower with spreading tips; opposite, heart-shaped leaves 3"–5" wide on downy stalks.
Height: 6"–12"　　　　　　　　　　　　　　　**Bloom Season:** April–May

In spring, lovely heart-shaped leaves of wild ginger hide the camouflaged jug-like flowers that hug the ground. When rubbed between the fingers, the leaves and roots have a faint ginger-like smell that is similar to that of the ginger spice plant that grows in tropical areas. The roots of wild ginger were dried, powdered, and used by early settlers as a substitute for true ginger to season foods, especially meats. The root was also sliced and then cooked into a sugary syrup and made into a candy or poured over hotcakes. Scientists have discovered that this plant contains aristolochic acid, which may cause cancer if ingested. The common name little brown jugs is often used to describe the flowers of another wild ginger relative, *Hexastylis arifolia*.

LARGEFLOWER HEARTLEAF GINGER
Hexastylis shuttleworthii
Birthwort family (Aristolochiaceae)
Quick ID: Urn-shaped, mottled reddish-brown flower up to 1½" wide, 3 large spreading lobes; heart-shaped to rounded, waxy, evergreen low-lying leaves, 2"–4" long, greenish-white branching veins, smooth margin.
Height: 1"–4"   **Bloom Season:** May–July

This curious flower is endemic to the Southern Appalachians. Even though you know it is here, it is still a challenge to find, as the thick fleshy flowers lie low to the ground, hidden beneath the heart-shaped leaves. Found in rich mountain forests of North Carolina, largeflower heartleaf, or Shuttleworth's ginger, prefers moist acidic habitats such as those where you also find great rhododendron (*Rhododendron maximum*). The evergreen leaves of the wild gingers in the genus *Hexastylis* separate these from their cousins in the *Asarum* genus, such as wild ginger (*Asarum canadense*). Also, the flowers of largeflower heartleaf are comparatively larger than those of other gingers. The species name, *shuttleworthii*, honors Edward Shuttleworth (1829–1909), who collected plants in South America.

BLUE COHOSH
Caulophyllum thalictroides
Barberry family (Berberidaceae)

Quick ID: Greenish-yellow to brownish flowers with 6 petals tinged purplish-brown; deep blue berrylike fruits held upright on stems; leaves with 3–5 lobes; bluish-green chalky "bloom" covering leaves and stem when fresh.

Height: 1'–3'   **Bloom Season:** April–June

The name blue cohosh is a bit confusing, as the spring-blooming flowers are dull greenish-yellow, but it is the blueberry-like fruits that led to the name. The common name cohosh is derived from an Algonquian word meaning "it is rough," referring to the textured root of the plant. Northern blue cohosh (*C. giganteum*) blooms about 2 weeks earlier; a third species in this genus resides in East Asia. Long used by Native Americans and later colonists and midwives, blue cohosh roots were soaked in water to form teas and tonics to treat many disorders, especially female conditions. Typically used to induce labor, current research has found that blue cohosh can cause abortion and neonatal strokes or heart damage.

FALSE HELLEBORE
Veratrum viride
Bunchflower family (Melanthiaceae)
Quick ID: Flowers clustered on 8"–20" stems at top of plant; star-shaped greenish-yellow hairy ½" wide flowers; large alternate, ribbed 6"–12" leaves that clasp the tall, stout stem.
Height: 2'–8'   **Bloom Season:** May–July

False hellebore is often found growing with skunk cabbage (*Symplocarpus foetidus*) in wet, marshy areas. Many plants, including false hellebore, protect themselves from herbivores with chemicals called alkaloids that are bitter and often toxic. Containing over 200 different alkaloids, all parts of false hellebore are highly toxic and cause severe vomiting, low blood pressure, and potentially death if ingested. The toxins in false hellebore have been used to kill rats, mice, and lice. Mothers dipped the family comb and brush in the plant's juice to kill head lice. In the 1940s it was used as a treatment for high blood pressure, but side effects included violent vomiting and nausea, and its use has been discontinued. You can see false hellebore and skunk cabbage in the wet areas at Mabry Mill.

APPALACHIAN BUNCHFLOWER
Veratrum parviflorum
Bunchflower family (Melanthiaceae)

Quick ID: Small bright yellowish-green flowers, 3 rounded petals and 3 rounded petal-like sepals (tepals), 6 stamens with yellow tips; oval basal leaves 4⁷⁄₁₀"–8⅗" long with narrower end at the base.

Height: 1'–5'   **Bloom Season:** July–September

The unique blossoms of bunchflowers are formed from three petals and three sepals that all look alike and are collectively termed tepals. Appalachian, or mountain, bunchflower is an unusual looking plant with a long thin central stem and thin side stems that hold the green flowers. Appalachian bunchflower is somewhat similar to false hellebore (*Veratrum viride*), but it has leaves all the way up the stem. Very slow to develop, some members of this genus can take up to forty years before becoming sexually mature. Look for this Southern Appalachian endemic near Heintooga Road. Members of this genus contain many toxic alkaloids, one of which, cyclopamine, is being studied in the treatment of brain, breast, and pancreatic cancers.

AUTUMN CORALROOT
Corallorhiza odontorhiza
Orchid family (Orchidaceae)

Quick ID: Tiny nondescript flowers ⅛" long, whitish with purplish-brown tips; leaves are overlapping sheathes hugging greenish-yellow unbranched stem; fruit is a pendulous egg-shaped capsule.

Height: 5"–8"   **Bloom Season:** August–October

Coralroot orchids are not one of the more striking members of the Orchid family. In fact, most people pass them by with hardly a second glance. Highly camouflaged against the forest floor, they are barely noticeable unless you look carefully. Three species of coralroot can be found growing along the Blue Ridge Parkway, each at a different season. The very similar spring, or Wister's, coralroot (*C. wisteriana*) blooms much earlier in the season, April–May, and has magenta spots on the lower lip. Blooming July–August, spotted coralroot (*C. maculata*) has dull brownish-purple flowers; the lower lip is white with red spots. Autumn coralroot is a plant that relies on underground fungi for nutrients.

SOLOMON'S SEAL
Polygonatum biflorum
Ruscus family (Ruscaceae)

Quick ID: Long arching stem; alternate, oval, 2"–6" leaves with obvious parallel veins; 1–3 greenish to white tubular, ½"–1" flowers dangle below stem, petals flare at base of tube; fruits are round green berries that ripen deep blue.

Height: 12"–48"   **Bloom Season:** April–June

Two rows of small bell-shaped greenish-white to cream flowers hang delicately from the long arching stem of Solomon's seal. The flower was named to honor King Solomon, who purportedly made use of many medicinal herbs. The horizontal underground stem, or rhizome, has marks that resemble the wax seal used on important documents. Native Americans ate the prepared rhizomes by roasting, frying, or beating them into flour to make bread. The leaves and young stems were eaten like greens. The plant was also used to treat dysentery, lung diseases, and as a salve for sores. A larger variety, King Solomon's seal, is a robust form that differs in chromosome number. Look for Solomon's seal throughout the Parkway, including along the Cascades Trail at E. B. Jeffress Park.

11

WOOD NETTLE
Laportea canadensis
Nettle family (Urticaceae)
Quick ID: Tiny greenish flowers in clusters; alternate serrated leaves; stout stem with stinging hairs.
Height: 1⅗'–4' **Bloom Season:** May–August

Wood nettle is often abundant in open woods, rich cove forests, and especially along streams and moist ditches along the Blue Ridge Parkway. Hikers along Parkway trails soon learn to avoid brushing up against this plant, as its stinging hairs can penetrate clothing. When brushed against, the tip of the stinging hairs breaks off, leaving a sharp point through which it injects irritating compounds including acetylcholine and histamine into the unfortunate victim, causing a painful stinging sensation that may last for hours or days. In the same family, stinging nettle (*Urtica dioica*) has opposite leaves. Soaking or cooking the leaves and young stems removes the stinging compounds. Quite nutritious, both plants can be boiled and eaten like spinach.

CHICORY
Cichorium intybus
Aster family (Asteraceae)
Quick ID: Flat flower with sky-blue squared, fringed petals, sometimes pink to white; hairy stem, irregularly toothed leaves.
Height: 10"–48"   **Bloom Season:** June–October

Often considered a weed, the pastel blue pinwheel flowers of chicory have one of the most significant accounts of all wildflowers. The plant was introduced into the New World from Europe, and thrifty settlers added 1 part chicory root to 2 parts coffee to stretch the morning brew. Soldiers in the Civil War and World War II used it as a coffee substitute. It's well known as a remedy for intestinal worms, and farmers who graze their herds in chicory-laden fields have healthier cattle. Chicory's versatility doesn't stop here—scientists have found that the deep taproot has antibacterial and anti-inflammatory properties. This "weed" may have future use for treating osteoarthritis, cardiovascular, and liver problems. Containing inulin, chicory is currently used as a sugar substitute and dietary fiber source.

ROBIN'S PLANTAIN
Erigeron pulchellus
Aster family (Asteraceae)
Quick ID: Over 60 thin, lavender, daisy-like petals, flowers have yellow center; hairy, soft stems; hairy leaves with bottom leaves flat as well as hairy.
Height: 8"–24"   **Bloom Season:** April–June

Along with the arching white-flowered branches of early-spring blackberry shrubs, the daisy-like flowers of Robin's plantain thrive in sunny open areas. Forming inviting blankets of pastel beauty at overlooks, Robin's plantain is one of the most common early-spring flowers along parkway roadsides and fields. Early-spring butterflies such as azures, hairstreaks, and skippers enjoy the 1"–1½" flat landing pad and refreshing nectar offered by the pinkish-lavender flowers. Widespread in the eastern states and Canada, the flowers of Robin's plantain are showier and larger than its fleabane relatives, such as common fleabane (*E. philadelphicus*), which sports smaller white-petaled flowers. Native Cherokee used this plant medicinally to treat headaches, colds, and coughs and mixed it with tallow to heal sores.

HOLLOW JOE-PYE WEED
Eutrochium fistulosum
Aster family (Asteraceae)
Quick ID: Pinkish-purple flowers in a large dense, round-topped cluster about 1' in diameter; smooth purplish hollow stem; lance-shaped 4"–12" leaves in whorls of 4–7 around the stem.
Height: 3'–10'   **Bloom Season:** July–October

If you enjoy watching butterflies, you should learn to recognize joe-pye weed, also known as trumpetweed. Found in wet areas throughout the eastern and central states, the pinkish-purple blooms of these tall flowers are butterfly magnets, attracting these flying jewels in throngs. Joe-pye weed is named for early New England herbalist Joe Pye, who used this plant to treat typhus, a bacterial disease carried by fleas and lice. Recently separated from *Eupatorium* into the *Eutrochium* genus, several other species of joe-pye weed can be found along the Parkway, including sweet joe-pye weed (*E. purpureum*), which has green stems with dark nodes, and the hairy stemmed Steele's joe-pye weed (*E. steelei*), which is a high-elevation Appalachian endemic.

HELLER'S BLAZING STAR
Liatris helleri
Aster family (Asteraceae)
Quick ID: Spike of lavender flowers with soft bristles; thin grasslike leaves.
Height: 6"–16"   **Bloom Season:** July–September

Being a member of a rare species club is not necessarily an honor, but Heller's blazing star is one such species. Placed on the federal threatened and endangered species list in 1987, it is known only from a handful of locations in the Blue Ridge Mountains. It requires high-elevation rock outcrops and grassy balds to survive. Blazing stars are sometimes commonly called gay feathers, button snakeroot, or rattlesnake master. Parkway botanists have worked hard to protect this special plant, which is threatened by trampling from hikers, climbers, and sightseers. Hikers and visitors to the park should respect this and other vulnerable plants and make sure to stay on trails, especially in these sensitive habitats.

DENSE BLAZING STAR
Liatris spicata
Aster family (Asteraceae)
Quick ID: Tall dense spike of reddish-purple tubular flowers with fringes; alternate long, narrow leaves.
Height: 2'–6'   **Bloom Season:** July–October

In late summer, the sunny meadows of Doughton Park are lushly decorated with lavender spikes of small tufted flowers waving merrily in the open fields. This eastern native thrives in the prairie-like habitat here along with butterfly milkweed (*Asclepias tuberosa*), tickseed (*Coreopsis* spp.), and mountain mints (*Pycnanthemum* spp.). Butterflies such as silver-spotted skippers are attracted to the nectar-rich blooms. Blazing stars, or gayfeathers, bloom from the top down and are popular as garden plants. Long known for their medicinal properties, blazing stars were used by Native Americans as a painkiller for backaches and as a remedy for swelling. It was also used to prevent colic and excess gas. Several other species can be found in the park, including tall gayfeather (*L. aspera*) and scaly gayfeather (*L. squarrosa*).

PURPLE STEM ASTER
Symphyotrichum puniceum
Aster family (Asteraceae)

Quick ID: Large clusters of whitish light blue to light violet flowers, outer ray petals surround yellow center (disk flowers) that turn brownish-purple with age; bristly, greenish-purple stems; rough, toothed, lance-shaped leaves.

Height: 2'–7'   **Bloom Season:** September–October

Along the Parkway, the commonly seen purple stem aster resembles the deeper purple flowers of New England aster (*S. novae-angliae*), which sometimes escapes from local flower gardens. Similar to purple stem aster, late purple aster (*S. patens*) has backward-curving bracts called phyllaries, but its leaf bases nearly encircle the stem. Smooth blue aster (*S. laeve*) has smooth greenish stems. Lowrie's aster (*S. lowrieanum*) has heart-shaped leaves with a winged stalk and a greasy feel. Appalachian clasping aster (*S. phlogifolium*) has characteristic very thin leaves that are pinched near the base. Also found in the park is wavy-leaved aster (*S. undulatum*), which has wavy heart-shaped leaves that clasp the stem.

RIGID WHITETOP ASTER
Symphyotrichum retroflexum
Aster family (Asteraceae)
Quick ID: Flowers have 13–30 purple ray petals, creamy yellowish-white center (disk flowers); green bract-like sepals (phyllaries) are turned backward (retroflexed); linear to elliptical leaves with serrated edges; robust stem is smooth below the flowers.
Height: 16"–39"   **Bloom Season:** August–October

Rigid whitetop aster is a large, showy aster found in mountainous areas of western North Carolina along the Blue Ridge Parkway. It begins blooming in late August and continues through fall into October. The pale purple flowers attract a large number of butterflies, including migrating monarchs on their journey south to Mexico. It is found in only three other Southern Appalachian states: Tennessee, South Carolina, and Georgia. Look for rigid whitetop aster at Milepost 377 and Mount Mitchell State Park. Based on DNA sequencing, many common asters in North America are now placed in the genus *Symphyotrichum* rather than the genus *Aster*. In many older wildflower field guides, rigid whitetop aster may be listed as *Aster retroflexus or A. curtisii*. These older names are known as synonyms.

NEW YORK IRONWEED
Vernonia noveboracensis
Aster family (Asteraceae)

Quick ID: Clusters of violet-purple flat-topped flower heads, each with 30–50 flowers; alternate, lance-shaped 4"–8" leaves; stiff, greenish-purple stems.

Height: 3'–7'   **Bloom Season:** July–September

To a butterfly, a field of the vivid violet-purple flowers of New York ironweed looks like a juicy candy store open and free for the taking. Native to the eastern states, New York ironweed blooms in late summer and fall. The genus name, *Vernonia*, honors Cambridge botanist and entomologist William Vernon (1680–1711), who studied and collected plants in Maryland in 1698. The species name, *noveboracensis*, means "of New York" and may refer to where the plant was first collected. Native Americans used ironweed to ease pain after childbirth. An infusion of the root was also used for loose teeth and for stomach ulcers.

VIRGINIA BLUEBELLS
Mertensia virginica
Borage family (Boraginaceae)
Quick ID: Buds pink; pale blue, nodding, 1" trumpet-shaped flowers; 2"–6" alternate, smooth, oval leaves; fragile stem.
Height: 1'–2'   **Bloom Season:** March–May

Under a canopy of April's flowering dogwood and redbud, the eye-catching pastel colors of Virginia bluebells form undulating carpets of baby-shower blues and pinks. Also called Roanoke bells or Virginia cowslip, the flowers put on an enjoyable knee-high show along low-elevation streams and riverbanks such as near the James River Visitor Center at Milepost 63.8. The pigments in the flowers change color depending on their pH. As the plant ages and becomes more alkaline, the pink buds change to pale blue, which helps attract pollinators such as butterflies and bees. A favorite woodland wildflower, Virginia bluebells was one of the first flowers Thomas Jefferson took note of in his 1766 garden observations near his home in Monticello, Virginia.

WILD COMFREY
Cynoglossum virginianum
Borage family (Boraginaceae)

Quick ID: Pale blue ³⁄₁₀"–²⁄₅" 5-petaled flowers in a rounded group atop hairy stem; thick, hairy 4"–8" long oval leaves at the base; hairy stem leaves are tapered and clasp stem.

Height: 1'–2' **Bloom Season:** May–June

In the same family as Virginia bluebells (*Mertensia virginica*), flowers of wild comfrey are pale sky blue and don't form the bell shape of bluebells. Also, the leaves and stem of wild comfrey are hairy in comparison to the smooth nature of Virginia bluebells. Native Americans used the root to treat cloudy urine. They boiled the root in water and applied the medicine to itching genitals. Because of its similar appearance to the common comfrey of Europe and Asia, early settlers used this plant in a comparable manner, eating the leaves like cooked spinach. Cancer and severe liver damage have been associated with herbal supplements and teas containing comfrey, as the plant contains dangerous toxins called pyrrolizidine alkaloids. Symptoms of abdominal distress may not appear for days after ingestion.

VIPER'S BUGLOSS
Echium vulgare
Borage family (Boraginaceae)
Quick ID: Tubular ¾" flowers start pink then turn bright blue, protruding red stamens; bristly hairs on lance-shaped leaves and stem; branched stem speckled with red spots.
Height: 12"–30"   **Bloom Season:** June–September

In late summer, motorists along the Blue Ridge Parkway may notice a spike of blue flowers growing in disturbed areas. A hardy introduction from Eurasia, viper's bugloss grows easily in dry meadows and fields. The genus name, *Echium*, is Greek for "viper" and refers to the shape of the seeds. *Bugloss* (pronounced BEW-gloss) is derived from the Greek word for the tongue of an ox, referring to the shape and roughness of the leaves. On sunny days the flowers are often loaded with hungry bees and butterflies, which relish the sweet nectar. Just as natives in the Southern Appalachians cherish honey derived from sourwood blooms, New Zealanders have discovered the golden light taste of viper's bugloss, or blue borage, honey.

APPALACHIAN BELLFLOWER
Campanula divaricata
Bellflower family (Campanulaceae)

Quick ID: Tiny bell-shaped blue flowers with long style; wiry stems; alternate, toothed, pointed 1"–3" leaves.

Height: 12"–24"   **Bloom Season:** July–October

Endemic to the Southern and Central Appalachians, wispy sprays of Appalachian bellflower cling tenaciously to rocky cliffs along the Blue Ridge Parkway. Also known as southern harebell, this beauty is distinguished by tiny blue bell-shaped flowers. True to its name, the petals of the tiny flowers are fused into a cup, the edges of which curl naturally backward. Upon close inspection, you will notice the long structure extending from the "bell" like an extended clapper, actually a section of the plant's female reproductive structure called a "style." At the proximal end, the ovary is protected within the cup; at the protruding end of the style is the sticky stigma, which catches pollen from visiting insects and hummingbirds.

GREAT BLUE LOBELIA
Lobelia siphilitica
Bellflower family (Campanulaceae)

Quick ID: Blue flowers on thick stem; tubular flowers about 1" long with a 2-lobed upper "lip" and projecting 3-lobed lower lip, white stripes underneath tube; alternate, toothed, oblong leaves.

Height: 2'–4'   **Bloom Season:** August–September

In late summer, scattered tall spikes of great blue lobelia decorate wet meadows and streambanks along the Blue Ridge Parkway. Even though all parts of the plant are poisonous, Native Americans used it for an extensive list of medical treatments. The Cherokee crushed the large leaves to use as a pain-relieving compress or poultice for headaches, boils, and sores. Like its bright red relative, cardinal flower (*L. cardinalis*), an infusion of great blue lobelia leaves was used to stop nosebleeds. An infusion of the roots or leaves was also used to treat worms, colds, rheumatism, fevers, and other ailments. The species name, *siphilitica*, refers to the plant's use as a hypothetical treatment for venereal disease.

25

ASIATIC DAYFLOWER
Commelina communis
Spiderwort family (Commelinaceae)
Quick ID: Flowers with 2 rounded blue petals and 1 small whitish petal, 6 yellow-tipped stamens; 3"–5" long lance-shaped leaves with bases that surround the stem.
Height: 4"–14"   **Bloom Season:** June–October

Few wildflowers lend themselves better to the imagination than common, or Asiatic, dayflower. This cartoonish flower sports 2 large, bright blue petals that perfectly resemble the prominent ears of Mickey Mouse. A third smaller petal is translucent bluish-white and insignificant in comparison with its showcased companions. Closing by midday, the bright blue petals contain clear cells that cause them to sparkle like miniature diamonds in sunlight. This dayflower has been introduced into North America and Europe from East Asia, where it is commonly known as "duck foot herb." Its bright blue flowers were used as a source of dye, especially for woodcarvings. Asiatic dayflower is considered a weed, often competing with native wildflowers for resources.

ZIGZAG SPIDERWORT
Tradescantia subaspera
Spiderwort family (Commelinaceae)
Quick ID: Three broadly rounded blue petals surround 6 bright yellow stamens; long, to 15", linear leaves with a lengthwise crease.

Height: 8"–24"   **Bloom Season:** April–July

Spiderwort is a native wildflower found from Virginia south to Florida and west to Missouri and Louisiana. The long grasslike leaves of spiderwort somewhat resemble a large green spider, and the word *wort* refers to a wildflower often used for medicinal purposes. The sap also somewhat resembles a sticky spider's web. The genus name, *Tradescantia*, honors John Tradescant, gardener of Charles I of England. Spiderworts are quite promiscuous, and various species hybridize freely when they are found growing together. Early settlers added this plant to beer and drank the mixture every day for a month, believing the concoction would be helpful in the treatment of spider bites. Virginia spiderwort (*T. virginiana*) and Ohio spiderwort (*T. ohiensis*) can also be found along the Parkway.

BALSAM MOUNTAIN GENTIAN
Gentiana latidens
Gentian family (Gentianaceae)
Quick ID: Bluish-purple flowers are closed; opposite leaves; stout stem.
Height: 12"–27½"   **Bloom Season:** September–October

The unusual flowers of closed, or bottle, gentians never open their petals, and most people think they are always displaying their buds. An ingenious mutualistic relationship has formed between these closed flowers and bumblebees. Most insects can't reach inside the tightly formed flower, but large bumblebees can easily force their way into the flower to reach the ample nectar. Balsam Mountain gentian has a very restricted range in the Balsam Mountain area south of Asheville. Until recently it was described as a variety of soapwort gentian (*G. saponaria*) but has been raised to specific rank. Other special endemics include Appalachian gentian (*G. decora*) (bottom inset), found at Julian Price Park, and Blue Ridge gentian (*G. austromontana*) (top inset), which can be found on grassy balds and forests at medium to high elevations.

STIFF GENTIAN
Gentianella quinquefolia
Gentian family (Gentianaceae)
Quick ID: Narrow, tubular with 4 ridges, lavender, upright, 1" flowers are pointed at the tip and appear closed; flowers in clusters at tips of stem; narrow to oval 1"–2½" stem leaves opposite, clasping the stem; stiff stems with 4 ridges.

Height: 8"–30"　　　　　　　　　　　**Bloom Season:** August–October

The lavender to violet tubular flowers of stiff gentian stand upright amid the goldenrods and asters of late summer. Stiff gentian can easily be distinguished from other purple gentians by its narrow flowers that are only about ¼" across and appear to have bristled lobes. Stiff gentian is sometimes called ague weed in reference to its use as a medicinal plant to reduce fevers. The word *ague* was a term used in the past to describe fevers or chills. The family name, Gentian, honors King Gentius of Illyria, who lived more than 2,000 years ago. He is credited as being the first person to discover the medicinal value of the European yellow gentian (*Gentiana lutea*).

WILD GERANIUM
Geranium maculatum
Geranium family (Geraniaceae)

Quick ID: 1¼" flowers with 5 pinkish-purple flat petals; leaves are deeply lobed into 5–6 parts.

Height: 8"–20"   **Bloom Season:** April–June

Most people are familiar with the geraniums that are often grown in gardens and window boxes, but wild geranium looks very little like its cultivated cousin. A common wildflower of eastern forests, the pinkish-purple flowers consist of 5 broad petals that curve slightly inward in a saucer shape. It is sometimes called cranesbill due to the bill-like seed case, hence the genus name, *Geranium*, which comes from the Greek word for crane. The tannin-rich roots of wild geranium have astringent properties and were used by Native Americans as a mouthwash for sore gums and teeth and also to help heal a childhood oral fungal disease called thrush. The pulverized root was also applied to soothe painful hemorrhoids. Look for wild geranium in open meadows and undisturbed roadsides along the Parkway.

CRESTED IRIS
Iris cristata
Iris family (Iridaceae)
Quick ID: Violet-blue, 2½"–6" wide flowers with 3 petals and 3 petal-like sepals with 3-ridged toothed, yellow crest with white border; broad, linear 4"–7" leaves sheath the slender stem.

Height: 4"–9"   **Bloom Season:** April–May

The lavender to violet-blue iris flowers of crested or crested dwarf iris are distinctly marked with a frilled white-and-yellow crest. These colorful stripes serve as nectar guides to channel pollinators into the nectar. In the 1750s John Bartram (1699–1777), who is sometimes called the "father of American botany," sent crested iris plants back to England for cultivation. The very similar dwarf iris (*I. verna*) (inset) lacks the crests on the sepals, and the leaves are narrower. Dwarf iris also is fragrant, while crested iris is only slightly fragrant or not at all. Blue flag (*I. versicolor*) and the introduced yellow flag (*I. pseudacorus*) are much taller, reaching up to 3', and are found in marshy areas.

31

BLUE-EYED GRASS
Sisyrinchium angustifolium
Iris family (Iridaceae)

Quick ID: Small ½" blue flowers with a yellow center, each petal (3 petals plus 3 sepals) tipped with a point; grasslike linear leaves are less than ¼" wide.

Height: 6"–20"   **Bloom Season:** March–June

With its grasslike leaves, finding blue-eyed grass is not an easy task. The small blue flowers with a yellow center sit atop a flat stem that blends in quite well with the surrounding grasses. The long parallel leaves identify it as a member of the Iris family. Native Americans cooked and ate the stems with other greens. An infusion of the root was given to children when they suffered from diarrhea. Interestingly, it was also used for constipation. Also found in the park, Atlantic blue-eyed grass (*S. atlanticum*) has a narrower main stem. Look for blue-eyed grass in open meadows in the park and along trails such as the Cascades Trail at E. B. Jeffress Park.

GILL-OVER-THE-GROUND
Glechoma hederacea
Mint family (Lamiaceae)

Quick ID: Pale blue-violet tubular snapdragon-like flowers, ½"–1" long, 2 upper lobes and 3 lower lobes, reddish spots inside; creeping 4-sided ground vine up to 16"; leaves opposite, evergreen, ½"–1½", rounded with scalloped edges, heavily veined; fruit brownish nutlets.

Height: 1"–8"   **Bloom Season:** April–July

Like many plants that were introduced from Europe, gill-over-the-ground, or ground ivy, has become naturalized in North America. Creeping along the ground, it often forms dense patches of tangled mats that when stepped on produce a pungent, earthy spice scent. Early settlers brought this plant with them from Europe, as it was highly valued for its many medicinal properties. They used it to treat headaches, wounds, and kidney problems. Rich in vitamin C, the leaves were made into a tea and used as a spring tonic and for coughs and colds. So powerful were its purported healing properties that it was boiled with white wine, mixed with oil, and rubbed onto the shaved head of a person to cure him or her of lunacy.

WILD BERGAMOT
Monarda fistulosa
Mint family (Lamiaceae)
Quick ID: Pale to bright lavender dense flower heads; reflexed tubular petals; square stems; opposite, serrated, hairy leaves.
Height: 1½'–4'   **Bloom Season:** April–August

Unlike its red cousin, scarlet beebalm (*M. didyma*), which likes to grow in moist areas, wild bergamot prefers a drier habitat. Many pollinators including bees, butterflies, and ruby-throated hummingbirds are attracted to the sweet nectar reward hidden deep within the tubular petals. A highly fragrant plant, the crushed leaves emit a pleasant citrusy-mint aroma that's apparently similar to the odor of oranges grown near Bergamo, Italy; hence the name bergamot. The genus name, *Monarda*, was given to honor Nicholás Monardes, an early Spanish herbalist who in the 1500s was the first to write about the newly discovered American plants. The species name, *fistulosa*, means "tubelike," describing the long curved flower parts. Look for wild bergamot blooming at Peaks of Otter and many other areas along the Parkway.

HEAL-ALL
Prunella vulgaris
Mint family (Lamiaceae)
Quick ID: Violet flowers on dense, squarish head, fringed lower lip, upper petal lip arching; opposite, oval, slightly toothed leaves; square stem.
Height: 3"–12"   **Bloom Season:** May–September

Heal-all, or self-heal, is a low or creeping plant that is found along road-sides and trails throughout the park. Introduced from Europe, this plant has been used for many folk remedies. Often overlooked, the plant has quite lovely small lilac-colored flowers that surround an elongated club-shaped head. Reminiscent of the shape of a tiny orchid, the exquisite flowers are pastel purple, hooded with a fringed lower lip that is often pale purple to whitish in color. Traditionally a tea was made from the leaves and used as a gargle for sore throats. The tea was also used for fevers and diarrhea. This small plant is sometimes confused with lousewort (*Pedicularis canadensis*), but the leaves of lousewort are highly dissected.

LESSER PURPLE FRINGED ORCHID

Platanthera psycodes

Orchid family (Orchidaceae)

Quick ID: Purple-magenta flowers on a spike; 3 fringed lobes on lower lip, base of flower lip dumbbell shaped; lance-shaped, alternate leaves up to 8" with parallel veins.

Height: 1'–3'   **Bloom Season:** June–July

Orchids are a favorite of many wildflower lovers, and the striking beauty of the lesser purple fringed orchid may take top prize. A close-up investigation divulges the intricacy of this exquisite blossom, revealing delicately fringed lower petals and a dumbbell-shape opening in the throat of the flower. The species name, *psycodes*, means "like a butterfly," referring to the spreading fringed petals. Two species of purple fringed orchid can be found along the Blue Ridge Parkway. The greater purple fringed orchid (*P. grandiflora*) has slightly larger flowers with a circle at the flower throat rather than the dumbbell shape of the lesser purple fringed species. These and other orchids are often the victims of plant poachers who inconsiderately pick these native beauties.

ALLEGHENY MONKEYFLOWER

Mimulus ringens
Lopseed family (Phrymaceae)

Quick ID: Lavender petals fused into a tube; flowers in pairs on long stalks in the leaf axil; 2 opposite, toothed, stemless leaves per node along the main square-ridged stem.

Height: 1'–3'　　　　　　　　　　　　　　　　**Bloom Season:** June–September

The snapdragon-like flowers of Allegheny monkeyflower have 2 bluish-purple upper lobes and 3 rounded lower lobes that when squeezed take on the appearance of a monkey's smiling face. Visitors from western states frequently enjoy many species of monkeyflower but may be surprised to find that there are only 2 species found in this region. Both Allegheny monkeyflower and the very similar winged monkeyflower (*M. alatus*) can be found in marshes, bogs, and wet meadows. Winged monkeyflower has flowers that are short-stalked, and the main stem has thin "wings" along the ridges. In August look for these monkeyflowers in wet areas including Rakes Mill Pond at Milepost 162 and Peaks of Otter at Milepost 86.

BLUE RIDGE BEARDTONGUE
Penstemon smallii
Plantain family (Plantaginaceae)

Quick ID: Purplish pink tubular flowers with white throat, 5 stamens, 1 of which has a small tuft of hairs; stems branched, with the flowering branches along the stem bushy looking, stem hairs short and fuzzy; opposite leaves, heart-shaped, clasp the stem; basal leaves turn reddish in winter.

Height: 16"–28"   **Bloom Season:** May–July

Endemic to the Southern Appalachians in North Carolina, Blue Ridge or Small's beardtongue occurs in open forests and along Parkway roadsides. These tubular flowers are often called "beardtongues" because of the small tuft of hairs on the sterile stamen. In Greek the word *penstemon* means "five stamens." Named for an early botanical explorer, John Kunkel Small (1869–1938), Blue Ridge beardtongue looks bushier than other beardtongues and blooms longer than most others. Look for Blue Ridge beardtongue at Mileposts 279 and 326. Also look for the more delicate appearing Appalachian beardtongue (*P. canescens*), which has long and short hairs, some of which are glandular.

SOUTHERN BLUE MONKSHOOD
Aconitum uncinatum
Buttercup family (Ranunculaceae)
Quick ID: Violet-blue hooded flowers clustered at the end of a weak stem; palm-shaped leaved up to 6" are divided into 3–5 toothed lobes.
Height: 2'–4'   **Bloom Season:** August–October

The blooms of southern blue monkshood look like a helmet or hood. The weak, flexible stems sometimes intertwine with nearby plants. A white Southern Appalachian species, trailing wolfsbane (*A. reclinatum*), is also found on the Parkway. Members of the *Aconitum* genus all produce an alkaloid toxin called aconitine that helps protect the plants from herbivores. Aconitine is one of the most deadly poisons known. Eating this plant causes nausea, numbness, burning, and, more importantly, heart arrhythmias leading to paralysis of the heart and respiratory centers. Also found along the Parkway, a similar flower, tall larkspur (*Delphinium exaltatum*), has a backward-pointing spur, as does dwarf larkspur (*D. tricorne*). Enjoy these beauties, but remember that it is illegal to pick flowers in the park.

PURPLE FLOWERING RASPBERRY
Rubus odoratus
Rose family (Rosaceae)

Quick ID: Bushy shrub; magenta rose-like 1"–2" flowers with yellow center; up to 10" leaves alternate, toothed, resembling maple leaves with 5 pointed lobes; reddish-brown stems with sticky hairs; red bowl-shaped fruits.

Height: 3'–6'   **Bloom Season:** June–August

Perhaps not as spectacular as the dramatic laurels and rhododendrons that epitomize the Blue Ridge Parkway, purple flowering raspberry is a relatively long-lasting shrub that adds color to the changing scenery. This is the only member of the Rose family that does not have divided leaves, instead boasting large maple-like leaves that spread up to 10" across. Purple flowering raspberry is a native of eastern North America and was used prolifically by Native Americans. The tart, dry berries can be eaten raw but were more frequently dried for winter use or made into pies or jellies. The large leaves were used medicinally to ease the pain of childbirth and for bowel complaints. They were also used as extra padding in shoes.

COMMON BLUETS
Houstonia caerulea
Madder family (Rubiaceae)
Quick ID: Tiny pale blue to whitish flowers about ½" across; yellow center surrounded by 4 petals; slender stems; opposite ½" leaves.

Height: 2"–6"   **Bloom Season:** April–July

In late spring, open areas along trails, grassy meadows, and picnic areas become awash in colonies of tiny sky-blue flowers. Four rounded petals surround a spot of yellow in the center of the flower, inviting bee flies to enjoy a sip of nectar. Bluets were traditionally called Quaker ladies, as they reminded people of bonnet-clad women chatting gaily at meetings. The Cherokee used an infusion of bluets as an aid for problems with bedwetting. At least 7 species of bluet can be found along the Blue Ridge Parkway. The uncommon Roan Mountain bluet (*H. montana*) occurs on nearby Roan and Grandfather Mountains. The genus name, *Houstonia*, honors Dr. William Houston (1695–1733), an early botanist who collected plants in Central America.

APPALACHIAN BLUET
Houstonia serpyllifolia
Madder family (Rubiaceae)
Quick ID: Group of tiny bright blue flowers; 4 blue petals with center yellow spot; branched, creeping stems with some erect stems; round to oval leaves less than ³⁄₁₀".
Height: 4"–8"   **Bloom Season:** April–June

When André Michaux first saw this bright blue mat of delicate flowers, he knew they were different from other bluets he had seen before. Some- times called creeping, mountain, or thyme-leaf bluets, the tiny flowers of Appalachian bluets are brighter blue than the more widespread com- mon bluets (*H. caerulea*). Bluets are sometimes called Quaker ladies or Quaker bonnets in reference to their likeness to a tiny assembly of women wearing grayish-blue bonnets. *Serpyllifolia* means "thyme-like," in refer- ence to the similarity of this bluet's leaves to those of the herb thyme (*Thymus serpyllum*). Appalachian bluets are so named because they are only found in the Appalachian Mountains from Pennsylvania to Georgia.

COMMON BLUE VIOLET
Viola sororia
Violet family (Violaceae)
Quick ID: Violet to blue flowers with whitish center, 5 petals with tufts of hairs on lateral petals; flowers arise directly from ground on stem; heart-shaped leaves.
Height: 4"–6"   **Bloom Season:** February–May

Violets are divided into two main types. If you look closely at the flower stem, it either comes directly out of the ground (termed "stemless") or the flower stem branches from another stem (termed "stemmed"). Common blue violets are one of the so-called stemless violets whose stem comes directly from the ground. Well named, common blue violets are one of the most common and widespread violets, ranging from the East Coast through the Midwest. Marsh blue violet (*V. cucullata*) is very similar to common blue violet but only grows in wet areas. If you look carefully at the throat, the lateral petals have club-like hairs. The leaves of southern wood violet (*V. hirsutula*) are silvery-green above and purplish below, with purplish veins.

BIRD'S-FOOT VIOLET
Viola pedata
Violet family (Violaceae)

Quick ID: Flowers 1"–1½" across; 5 petals vary from pale blue to dark purple; 2 upper petals smaller than the lower 3 petals, lowest petal with dark streaking; 5 stamens with bright orange anthers; fan-shaped leaves are cut deeply into 3–5 segments with narrow lobes.

Height: 4"–10"   **Bloom Season:** April–June

The attractive multicolored petals of bird's-foot violet make it one of the loveliest of all spring wildflowers. Sometimes referred to as the diva of violets, bird's-foot violet is quite particular about its surroundings. It flourishes only in sunny areas with well-drained dry, sandy soils and is often associated with reindeer lichen (*Cladonia* spp.) in this habitat. The unusual segmented leaves make this one of the easiest violets to identify, as they are reminiscent of the foot of a bird. Two color forms may be found. The petals may be all the same light purple, or the upper 2 petals may be dark purple with the lower 3 petals pale violet. The seeds of this violet contain a sugary gel that attracts ants, which aid in dispersal.

WAVY LEAVED VIOLET
Viola subsinuata
Violet family (Violaceae)
Quick ID: Purple flowers with 5 petals; all leaf blades are lobed, with shallower sinuses toward the margins; the middle lobe is cleft.
Height: 3"–6"   **Bloom Season:** April–May

All the leaves of wavy leaved violet are lobed. Wavy leaved violet is very similar to early blue violet (*V. palmata*), but wavy leaved violet always has lobed leaves from the beginning. *V. palmata* has several common names, including wood violet, three-lobed violet, and tri-lobed violet. Common names can be confusing, as other violets can commonly be called wood violet, including southern woodland violet (*V. hirsutula*). Early blue violet also has many synonyms, including *V. palmata* var. *triloba*, *V. falcata*, and *V. triloba*, most of which refer to its lobed leaves. Early blue violet has unlobed early leaves followed by lobed ones. Arrowleaf violet (*V. sagittata*) has arrow-shaped leaves that are often purplish below and jaggedly toothed at the base. The young leaves may be heart-shaped.

NODDING WILD ONION
Allium cernuum
Onion family (Alliaceae)
Quick ID: Nodding ball of bell-shaped pink to whitish lavender flowers at end of stalk; stem crooks at end; thin, linear leaves.
Height: 1'–2' **Bloom Season:** July–August

Delicate sleepy heads of nodding wild onion emerge along the trails and roadsides in midsummer. The tiny bell-shaped pink to whitish lavender flowers hang in a cluster from the single drooping stem, so pollinators such as bees must hang upside down to reach the nectar. Like all onions, the stem and flower arise from an underground bulb that smells oniony, lending the same flavor to the milk of cows that eat the leaves. Mountain families dug the bulbs to fry in lard or added it to soups stews. Used medicinally, an onion poultice was placed on the chest of children who were sick with a cough or the croup. The Algonquian name for this flower was *chigagou*, from which came the name for the city of Chicago.

COMMON MILKWEED
Asclepias syriaca
Dogbane family (Apocynaceae)
Quick ID: Pinkish flowers in round clusters with 5 reflexed petals, oval opposite leaves hairy underneath; milky sap; fruits are dry, brown, elongated pods that split, releasing silky tufts attached to seeds.
Height: 3'–5'   **Bloom Season:** June–August

Wild animals learn to avoid eating milkweeds at a young age, as these plants contain a milky-looking sap containing bitter toxic chemicals. Monarch butterflies have evolved with milkweeds, accumulating the toxins in their bodies as added protection from bird predators. Native Americans used the root of milkweeds as a treatment for pleurisy and other lung ailments leading to the name pleurisy root. Several species of milkweed can be found along the Parkway, including poke milkweed (*A. exaltata*), which sports loosely formed whitish flower heads. Wildlife and nature lovers can aid the decreasing populations of monarchs by planting milkweeds in their home gardens. Make sure to purchase the seeds or plants from a reputable dealer—digging milkweeds from the wild reduces their natural populations.

SWAMP THISTLE
Cirsium muticum
Aster family (Asteraceae)
Quick ID: Pink bristly-looking flowers; branching stems; alternate leaves, elliptic, 4"–10" and deeply lobed, weakly spiny; feathery appendages on seeds.
Height: 3'–7'   **Bloom Season:** July–November

Due to the introduction of several invasive species from Eurasia, thistles have been undeservedly marked as prickly, noxious weeds that should be eradicated, but native species are quite beautiful. Thistles lack showy ray flowers, such as the white "petals" of daisies. The rosy-pink blossoms are disk flowers common to the Aster family. Thistles are butterfly magnets and are super plants on which to spot these colorful insects. Perhaps using the first hair-loss treatment, the ancient Roman naturalist Pliny applied a decoction of thistles to restore hair to a balding head. Along with swamp thistle, 3 other species of thistle can be found along the Blue Ridge Parkway. Tall thistle (*C. altissimum*) and field thistle (*C. discolor*) are also native plants; the introduced bull thistle (*C. vulgare*) is a weedy pest.

DAME'S ROCKET
Hesperis matronalis
Mustard family (Brassicaceae)
Quick ID: Bright pink to white flowers clustered at top of stem, 4 petals; alternate lance-shaped, toothed, 2"–6" leaves.
Height: 1'–3'   Bloom Season: April–August

A showy plant with an unusual name, dame's rocket, or dame's violet, has large clusters of fragrant flowers with variable pink to white petals. A member of the Mustard family, it resembles a phlox except that it has 4 petals instead of the phlox's 5 petals. Early settlers brought this central and southern European native with them to the New World in the 1600s. During the day these flowers smell somewhat like violets, but near evening they perfume the air with a sweet, clove-like odor. The species name *matronalis* means "dame" or "matron," referring to the March 1 Roman festival that celebrated married women. *Rocket* is from a similar plant grown in the Mediterranean region called rocket, or arugula, which is used for salads.

DEPTFORD PINK
Dianthus armeria
Pink family (Caryophyllaceae)
Quick ID: Hot pink flowers, 5 notched petals with white dots; grasslike leaves.
Height: 6"–24"   **Bloom Season:** May–September

Related to the carnations and sweet William often planted in gardens, Deptford pink is a small plant with hot pink flowers. The petals are dotted with white spots, which tend to make the flower glow like raindrops in the sun. Introduced from Europe, this energetic plant has spread throughout most of North America and thrives in disturbed areas and along roadsides. Because the leaves and slight stems resemble a grass, this plant is sometimes called grass pink. The common name refers to Deptford, England, an area of southeast London. In 1633 herbalist Thomas Johnson named the plant for this area, but the plant that he found was probably maiden pink (*D. deltoides*). Botanical rules state that the first name given to a plant sticks; therefore, the imposter was so named.

BOUNCING BET
Saponaria officinalis
Pink family (Caryophyllaceae)

Quick ID: Pale pink 1" wide flowers, 5 petals with square notched ends, petals spread and slightly flair backward; smooth branching stems; opposite smooth oval 2"–3" leaves with obvious veins.

Height: 1'–2'   **Bloom Season:** June–September

Traveling across the ocean from Europe, early settlers brought seeds of familiar and useful plants from their gardens to the New World. One of these favorite plants was a member of the Pink family called soapwort or, more commonly, bouncing Bet. Soapwort contains a substance known as saponin, which produces a soapy froth when agitated in water. Not only was the foam used to clean hands and clothing, it also was added to flat beer to produce a nice frothy head. The phlox-like petals of this sweet-smelling flower are recurved, not unlike the hitched-up skirts of a washerwoman bending up and down over her washboard. Forming loose colonies, the pale pink flowers can be seen in fields and disturbed areas.

ALLEGHENY STONECROP
Hylotelephium telephioides
Stonecrop family (Crassulaceae)
Quick ID: Light pink star-shaped flowers in clusters, 5 pointed petals, stamens pink tipped; opposite, thick, fleshy, leaves are oval.
Height: 7"–18" **Bloom season:** July–September

Along the Blue Ridge Parkway, Allegheny stonecrop, or Allegheny live-for-ever, flowers in late summer and fall. An inhabitant of rocky outcrops at mid to high elevations up to 6,500', this fuzzy looking pink flower has an amazing ability to withstand extreme conditions. Exposed to the harsh elements of cliff faces, its thick roots and succulent oval leaves store water to resist the drying effects of wind and sun. This plant is primarily found in the Central and Southern Appalachians. The species name, *telephioides*, means "resembling *Telephium*," for Telephus, the son of Hercules. Like many wildflowers that make their home on cliffs, these are subject to trampling by unwary hikers. Please be aware of these and other plants, especially in these extreme high-altitude conditions.

TRAILING ARBUTUS
Epigaea repens
Heath family (Ericaceae)
Quick ID: Fragrant whitish-pink flowers with 5 lobes; oval evergreen leaves; trailing woody stems have reddish hairs.
Height: 1"–2"   **Bloom Season:** March–May

This brave little flower blooms just as the ground is beginning to thaw in very early spring. This low creeping plant is a member of the Heath family, along with the rhododendrons and azaleas that tower above their diminutive cousin. The leathery evergreen leaves remain all year, but the pink flowers bloom only in the earliest spring months as one of the opening acts of the spring flower show. Trailing arbutus prefers sandy or rocky woodland areas with dry, acidic soils. The sweet spicy-scented flowers have a fresh alluring perfume similar to that of pure laundry detergent used for babies. Look for trailing arbutus along many trails in the park, including Cascades Trail at E. B. Jeffress Park.

SAND MYRTLE
Kalmia buxifolia
Heath family (Ericaceae)
Quick ID: Evergreen shrub, low-growing; small, shiny oval leaves; white to pink flowers with extruded stamens; bark shreds.
Height: 4"–39"   **Bloom Season:** March–June

Sand myrtle has a disjunct distribution in North Carolina, where it is found on the coastal plain pine barrens and in the southeastern Blue Ridge Mountains. It is not found in Virginia. The tiny pinkish-white flowers grow on high mountaintop heath balds in western North Carolina. You can see this lovely flower at 4,500' elevation along Rough Ridge Trail, where trampling by unaware hikers is a threat to this low-growing species. Make sure to stay on the boardwalk that was built to help protect the sand myrtle that grows here on the bald.

MOUNTAIN LAUREL
Kalmia latifolia
Heath family (Ericaceae)
Quick ID: Shrub; leathery pointed evergreen leaves, 2"–5" long and 1"–2" wide; bowl-shaped pink flowers; woody gnarled stems with furrows and ridges sloughing in narrow strips or flakes; basal burl.

Height: 6'–10'   **Bloom Season:** May–June

The bowl-shaped pastel pink flowers of mountain laurel can be seen in dense patches along the Blue Ridge Parkway. Mountain laurel is locally known as "ivy," while rhododendrons are referred to as "laurel." Large, thick patches of mountain laurel came to be called laurel "hells" or "slicks," as it is difficult to pass through the tangled branches without crawling. The burls that form at the base of the shrub were used to carve pipe bowls for smoking tobacco. Named for botanist Asa Gray (1810–1888), grayanotoxin is found in the leaves, flowers, and nectar of mountain laurel and other rhododendrons.

Honey collected from bees that have visited mountain laurel and rhododendron flowers is bitter. Because the toxin can cause nausea and slow heartbeats, beekeepers discard what they call "mad honey."

APPALACHIAN PYGMY PIPES
Monotropsis odorata
Heath family (Ericaceae)
Quick ID: Reddish-purple tubular flowers, petals with whitish pointed tips, often hidden by papery brown bracts; fleshy purplish brown stem.
Height: 2"–4"   **Bloom Season:** February–April

An unusual little flower, Appalachian pygmy pipes, or sweet pinesap, grows in rich forests in southeastern states, especially in Virginia and North Carolina. Blending in well with the leaf litter and pine needles along Parkway trails, such as the trail to Rattlesnake Lodge, they perfume the surrounding air with a very strong spicy odor of cloves. The small flowers require an acidic environment and are often found under or near mountain laurel (*Kalmia latifolia*) or great rhododendron (*Rhododendron maximum*). Appalachian pygmy pipes depend on a mutualistic relationship with an underground fungus for nutrients. In an unusual flowering pattern, the plant normally flowers in early spring, but can also bloom in September–November, when it lacks any odor at all.

CAWTABA RHODODENDRON
Rhododendron catawbiense
Heath family (Ericaceae)
Quick ID: Tall evergreen shrub; deep pink, large funnel-shaped flowers, 5" across; thick, alternate 3"–6" oblong leaves that are dark green above and light green to whitish below.
Height: 6'–10'   **Bloom Season:** May–June

Visitors from across the country come to the Blue Ridge Parkway in June to revel in the beauty of the native Catawba rhododendrons. Depending on the elevation and weather conditions, the dramatic pink show begins in mid-May into June. At higher elevations such as at Craggy Gardens, the blooms typically reach their peak in early to mid-June. In Virginia the rhododendron displays can be seen at Mount Rogers. The annual Rhododendron Festival is held in Roan Mountain State Park, Tennessee, which is 20 miles west of Banner Elk, North Carolina. A smaller species, Carolina rhododendron (*R. carolinianum*) (inset) is a Southern Appalachian endemic found at high altitudes along the Parkway from the Linville Gorge area south and west to the Great Smoky Mountains.

57

PINXTER AZALEA
Rhododendron periclymenoides
Heath family (Ericaceae)
Quick ID: Small to medium shrub; clusters of pale pink, tubular flowers with long protruding stamens; 2"–4" oval leaves.
Height: 4'–6'   **Bloom Season:** March–May

Pinxter azalea, or pinxter flower, is one of the earliest rhododendrons to bloom along the Parkway. *Pinxter* comes not from its pink coloration but from the Dutch word for Pentecost as the plant bloomed near this holiday. Pinxter flower is known for the 5 long, protruding stamens and 1 pistil in the large pink funnel-shaped flowers. A shrub of mountainous areas, it can be found from New York south through the Appalachians into Georgia.

Large pale green galls, caused by a fungus called *Exobasidium vaccinii,* are common on the branch tips and leaves of pinxter flower. The galls, called honeysuckle apples or mayapples, were pickled in vinegar and eaten as a delicacy. In some field guides, this species will be found under the old name, *R. nudiflorum.*

PINKSHELL AZALEA
Rhododendron vaseyi
Heath family (Ericaceae)

Quick ID: Deciduous shrub; light pink, bell-shaped flowers; stems leafless when blooming; alternate elliptical leaves, 1½"–5" long, widest near the middle and tapering to a point.

Height: 8'–12'   **Bloom Season:** May–June

From a distance, the rounded clusters of pink blooms look like cotton candy puffs displayed at a fair. Growing at elevations of 3,000'–5,500', the light pink bell-shaped flowers of pinkshell azalea bloom before the leaves are fully formed. Native to only a few counties in North Carolina, pinkshell azalea is a rare Appalachian endemic shrub. Pinkshell azalea was first documented in 1878 near Webster, North Carolina, by George R. Vasey, son of George S. Vasey, the first director of the US National Herbarium. A species of concern, threats come from habitat loss and illegal collection of plants from the wild. Pinkshell azalea occurs along the Blue Ridge Parkway from around the Grandfather Mountain area south to Great Smoky Mountains National Park.

GROUNDNUT
Apios americana
Pea family (Fabaceae)
Quick ID: Rounded clusters of reddish-brown to pinkish, ½" pealike flowers on hairy vine; intricate petals, rounded upper, sides winged and curved down, lower 2 petals sickle shaped; alternate leaves, 5 egg-shaped leaflets.

Height: Vine to 10'   **Bloom Season:** June–August

Stunning beauties, groundnuts have richly colored helmet-like flowers held by a twining vine that drapes over other plants. Found east of the Rocky Mountains in riparian woods and low damp bottomlands, groundnut is a widespread plant with underground potato-like tubers. Some interesting common names have been bestowed upon this plant, including wild potato, Virginia potato, Indian potato, ground potato, wild bean, and, locally, hopniss. Groundnut was an important source of food for Native Americans and early colonists. The underground tubers can be cooked and eaten like potatoes, and the beans that develop from the flowers are prepared like peas. The tubers were also dried and stored for winter use. Also in the Pea family, hog peanut (*Amphicarpaea bracteata*) (inset) is a similar pale pink–flowered vine but has 3 leaflets.

WILD BLEEDING HEART
Dicentra eximia
Fumitory family (Fumariaceae)
Quick ID: Deep pink, heart-shaped flowers hang down from curved stems, 4 petals connected at the base, 2 outer petals are bent backward; finely cut dissected leaves.
Height: 10"–18"   **Bloom Season:** April–July

Although you might think this uniquely heart-shaped flower came directly from a florist shop, wild bleeding heart is native to the Appalachian Mountains. Its cousin, Pacific bleeding heart (*D. formosa*) grows in coastal western states. The two are sometimes hybridized in nurseries to sell as attractive garden plants. Wild bleeding heart grows on rocky outcrops, cliffs, and talus slopes such as those on Sharp Top Mountain at Peaks of Otter. In the same family, the audaciously colored pink corydalis (*Capnoides sempervirens*) is the only member of its genus in North America. The bright pink tubular flowers terminate in yellow lips, leading to another common name, rock harlequin.

61

SWAMP PINK
Helonias bullata
Swamp Pink family (Heloniadaceae)

Quick ID: Dense cluster of small pink flowers, blue anthers; basal evergreen 3"–10" leaves are lance-shaped, stem leaves are reduced small bracts; stout, hollow stem.

Height: 1'–3'   **Bloom Season:** April–May

The unusual bright pink bottlebrush-like flower heads of swamp pink display an unusual beauty in the marshy areas they inhabit. Growing in acidic, wet soils, these plants prefer semi-shaded seepage areas that are constantly moist but not flooded. This rare flower is the only member of its genus in North America; its closest relatives reside in East Asia. So unique is this flower that in 1988 it was added to the threatened and endangered list for both Virginia and North Carolina. The few populations of swamp pink are threatened by habitat loss, pollution, and wetland drainage. Unscrupulous plant collectors and careless hikers also threaten the plant's existence. The Blue Ridge Parkway helps protect these special habitats and ecological communities.

BEADLE'S MOUNTAIN MINT
Pycnanthemum beadlei
Mint family (Lamiaceae)
Quick ID: Small lavender flowers in dense clusters; square hairy stems; opposite elliptic leaves are slightly serrated.
Height: 20"–35"   **Bloom Season:** August–September

With their characteristic square stems and minty odor, at least 8 of the 20 to 25 species of native North American mountain mint can be found along the Parkway, including Beadle's mountain mint. The various species are challenging to identify, as they sometimes hybridize and don't always conform to standard growth habits. Some species arise from the hybridization of other plants, and botanists are studying flowers such as Beadle's mountain mint, which is postulated to be a hybrid of two others, Appalachian mountain mint (*P. montanum*) and short-toothed mountain mint (*P. muticum*). This Appalachian endemic honors Canadian-born botanist Chauncey Delos Beadle (1866–1950), who established the Biltmore Herbarium, which at one time held over 100,000 specimens of plants before they were donated to the Smithsonian Institution.

SPRING BEAUTY
Claytonia virginica
Montia family (Montiaceae)

Quick ID: Flowers with 5 white oval petals, veins streaked with pink stripes, 4–13 flowers in a loose cluster; weak branching stems; 2"–5" flat, linear leaves.

Height: 3"–9"   **Bloom Season:** March–May

One of the earliest flowers to bloom, spring beauty often forms soft pink carpets on the warming forest floors. The genus, *Claytonia*, is named to honor John Clayton (1686–1773), a physician and early plant collector in Virginia. The genus has recently been moved from the Portulacaceae to the Montiaceae family. On the roots are small rounded potato-like structures called tubers, about ½"–2" in diameter. These small tubers were relished by Native Americans and then early colonists, who roasted or boiled them like potatoes. Due to the tubers' small size, it takes a lot of plants to make a meal, leading to one common name of fairy spuds. Another species, Carolina spring beauty (*C. caroliniana*), typically grows at higher elevations and has broader, diamond-shaped leaves.

PINK LADY'S SLIPPER
Cypripedium acaule
Orchid family (Orchidaceae)

Quick ID: Single pink, 2" pouch-shaped flower with slit in front; leafless stalk; 2 basal opposite leaves, 4"–10" long, oval with grooves.

Height: 6"–15" **Bloom Season:** April–June

Orchids are some of nature's most interesting flowers, captivating those who find them. Just like a human face, orchids have bilateral symmetry. Living a delicate symbiotic relationship with a very particular fungus, these plants take more than 10 years to produce a bloom. Native Americans used the roots of lady's slippers to make a tonic for worms. The roots have also been used as a substitute for the European plant valerian, which is used to treat nervous conditions, and is sometimes called "American valerian." In the nineteenth century the root was dried, powdered, and steeped in boiling water and then sold as a tranquilizing tonic. Take pleasure in these beautiful orchids, but please leave them for others to enjoy.

SHOWY ORCHIS
Galearis spectabilis
Orchid family (Orchidaceae)

Quick ID: Purplish-pink hood covers white lower lip petal of 1" flowers, 2–15 per stem; 2 wide, smooth, oval lower leaves, 4"–8", clasp the stem.

Height: 3"–10"   **Bloom Season:** April–June

Spring hikers on Blue Ridge Parkway trails often stop to appreciate the beauty and sweet scent of showy orchis. A member of the Orchid family, the flower's petals and sepals have converged to form a pink hood that covers the white, notched lower lip petal. Bumblebees appreciate the easy landing pad and, in the process of seeking nectar, collect the orchid's package of pollen to distribute to the next showy orchis for pollination. The tiny dustlike seeds that are later produced have no energy reserves and rely on certain underground fungi to germinate. In this unique association, called a mycorrhizal relationship, the fungus provides a source of nutrition for the tiny seed until it is big enough to photosynthesize on its own.

MOUNTAIN WOOD SORREL
Oxalis montana
Wood sorrel family (Oxalidaceae)
Quick ID: White flowers with pink stripes and hue, 5 notched petals with yellow dots toward middle; 3 clover-like leaves with 2 lobes.

Height: 3"–6" **Bloom Season:** May–July

Mountain wood sorrel flowers are perfectly suited to be stained-glass models—the 5 white petals display delicately line-drawn pink stripes leading to a central circle of pink arches over yellow dots. The flowers of spring beauty (*Claytonia* spp.) are very similar, but the shamrock-like leaves of the wood sorrel easily distinguish this plant. Some flowers such as mountain wood sorrel bloom only at high altitudes in forests dominated by spruce and firs. You can see mountain wood sorrel blooming along the Richland Balsam Trail. At lower altitudes, several other members of this genus can be found along the Parkway, including violet wood sorrel (*O. violacea*). Yellow-flowered wood sorrels include great yellow wood sorrel (*O. grandis*), Dillen's wood sorrel (*O. dillenii*), and common yellow wood sorrel (*O. stricta*).

APPALACHIAN TURTLEHEAD
Chelone lyonii
Plantain family (Plantaginaceae)

Quick ID: Deep rose-purple flowers with 2 lips, lower lip has tiny yellow hairs; opposite, oval to lance-shaped serrated leaves, 3"–5", widest below middle; leaves on ½"–1½" stalk (petiole).

Height: 16"–40" **Bloom Season:** July–September

The curiously shaped 2-lipped flowers of Appalachian turtlehead are conversation starters for wildflower lovers everywhere. Is it a turtle? Is it a snake? Perhaps a small pink shell lost far from the ocean? The genus name, *Chelone*, means "turtle"; the species name, *lyonii*, honors John Lyon (1765–1814), a botanist in the early nineteenth century. Always found in wet areas, turtlehead needs plenty of water to survive and can usually be found growing along with the orange or yellow wetland flowers spotted or pale jewelweed and the brilliant scarlet red flowers of cardinal flower. Other species of turtlehead can be found along the Parkway, including Cuthbert's turtlehead (*C. cuthbertii*) and mountain purple or red turtlehead (*C. obliqua*), both of which are pink. White turtlehead (*C. glabra*) sports white flowers.

CAROLINA PHLOX
Phlox carolina
Phlox family (Polemoniaceae)
Quick ID: Pink to lavender, 1" long, tubular flowers, 5 spreading petals that slightly overlap, squared ends, sometimes white streaks in center, yellow stamens; opposite, lanceshaped, 2"–5" leaves.
Height: 24"–30"   **Bloom Season:** May–August

Most gardeners are familiar with the showy garden phlox flowers sold in greenhouses. Carolina phlox, or thick leaf phlox, is the wild parent of many of these garden cultivars. A native, Carolina phlox grows wild in woodlands and forest edges, such as along trails at Craggy Gardens. Butterflies and moths use their long tongues to delve deep into the tubular lavender-pinkish flowers. Blooming about the same time as Carolina phlox another lookalike, smooth phlox (*P. glaberrima*), has petals that are more rounded or slightly bell-shaped. Blooming later, July–September, fall or garden phlox (*P. paniculata*) is another species that has been cultivated for garden flowers.

MOSS PHLOX
Phlox subulata
Phlox family (Polemoniaceae)

Quick ID: Creeping mats of pastel blue, pink, or pinkish-white ¾" wide flowers, 5 notched petals; opposite, needlelike ½"–1" leaves.

Height: 2"–6"   **Bloom Season:** April–May

Spreading mats of the pastel flowers of moss phlox hug the warm ground in early spring. Also known as moss pink or mountain pink, the 5 petals in a pinwheel happily soak up the warm rays of sun before they quickly fade away. The species name, *subulata*, is from the Latin word for "awl-shaped," referring to the slightly curved thin, needlelike leaves. The word *phlox* comes from a Greek word meaning "as a flame," referring to the colorful flowers. Bees, butterflies, and other early-flying spring insects visit the colorful flowers, seeking a sip of sweet nectar. Bright cultivars are often planted as ground cover in rock gardens or dry areas. Sometimes known as sticky catchfly, wild pink (*Silene caroliniana*) (right) is sometimes confused with phlox, but the petals are not fused as they are in members of the Phlox family.

GAYWINGS
Polygala paucifolia
Milkwort family (Polygalaceae)
Quick ID: Rosy-pink flowers with fringed tip, 2 oval winged sepals; alternate, oval ⅗"–1⅗" leaves
Height: 3"–6"   **Bloom Season:** April–June

Colonies of bright rosy-pink flowers boast 2 flaring petal-like sepals and a fringed lip that draw attention to this unusual plant found in moist rich woods. The exceptional shape has led to many common names, including gaywings, fringed polygala, and bird-on-the-wing. Blooming in spring, the flowers occur in clusters that resemble assemblies of small pink butterflies. It is a member of the Milkwort family; most of the members of this unpretentious family resemble baby bottle brushes. It was thought that eating these plants would increase the milk production of nursing mothers or cows. Ants collect the ripe seeds to eat the attached food body, called an elaiosome. The discarded seed is then able to start a new plant if germination occurs.

ROUND-LOBED HEPATICA
Anemone americana
Buttercup family (Ranunculaceae)
Quick ID: Flowers with 5–12 petals (petal-like sepals) ranging from pink to blue, white, lavender; flower heads 1" across; rounded 3-lobed leaves; stalks hairy.
Height: 4"–6"   **Bloom Season:** February–May

Hepaticas, or liverworts, are among the first harbingers of spring, bounding to life just as the warming springtime air breathes life into the forest. In rich woodlands the fallen brown leaves from the previous fall are often covered in an array of pastel as the flowers of liverwort range widely with pink, lavender, light blue, and white in gentle patches. The word *hepatic* refers to the liver, and the leaves of this plant are indeed liver-shaped. Following the "Doctrine of Signatures," early physicians believed that plants that resembled human body parts had useful relevance to those parts. Another species that can be found on the Blue Ridge Parkway, sharp-lobed hepatica (*Hepatica nobilis*) (inset) has sharply pointed rather than rounded leaves.

LEATHER FLOWER
Clematis viorna
Buttercup family (Ranunculaceae)
Quick ID: Urn-shaped reddish-purple leathery flowers on sprawling vine; leaves with 3–9 narrowly oval leaflets.
Height: 6'–18'   **Bloom Season:** May–September

The vines of leather flower climb gracefully over fences and small bushes, producing flowers in summer that sport graceful reddish-purple flowers. Leather flower is sometimes called vasevine, as the flowers hang like upside-down flower vases or urns along the vine. The 4 reddish-purple sepals are tough and leathery, hence the name leather flower. The genus name, *Clematis*, is from an ancient Greek word that means "a climbing plant." Another member of this genus, virgin's bower (*C. virginiana*), has starry white flowers that bloom along a vine in late summer. Their seeds have long, silky, curved plumes that drape fall shrubbery in a lacy frock. These inflated clusters of whitish feathery puffs resemble an old man's beard and are quite noticeable along the Parkway.

ROAN MOUNTAIN BLUET
Houstonia montana
Madder family (Rubiaceae)

Quick ID: Pink to reddish-purple, tubular flowers with 4 petals; opposite, oval leaves are rounded at the base and pointed toward the tip.

Height: 4"–12"   **Bloom Season:** April–June

Roan Mountain bluet is one of the many rare plants that is protected on Grandfather Mountain, just off the Blue Ridge Parkway. Located on only a few of the highest peaks in North Carolina, there are only about 12 known populations of this brave bluet in the world. Inspired by the early explorations of nearby Roan Mountain by André Michaux and Thomas Nuttall, it was famous botanist Asa Gray who first named this flower in 1841. The delicate pink flowers only grow on gravelly cliffs and exposed slopes on high-altitude balds. Unaware hikers and climbers threaten this special little plant by trampling on its tender stems. Roan Mountain bluet was added to the federal endangered species list in 1990.

BASHFUL WAKEROBIN
Trillium catesbaei
Trillium family (Trilliaceae)
Quick ID: Pink or white, 1⅖"–2⅕" flowers with 3 sharply backward curving petals that are wavy, outward curved yellow anthers, pale greenish ovary; whorl of 3 oval leaves roll inward and tend to be widely spaced apart.
Height: 8"–20"   **Bloom Season:** April–June

The flower is often rosy or pink, but when it is found in a white form, or white morph, it can be similar to southern nodding trillium (*T. rugelii*), which has dark anthers, whereas bashful wakerobin has anthers the color of egg yolk. All trilliums can be described as either having the flower sit directly on top of the leaves or having the flower on a stem held either above or below the petals. The flowers of this well-named plant hang bashfully below the characteristic 3 leaves. Wakerobin is a name that is applied to many species of trillium, as they tend to bloom when the American robins return in spring. The species name, *catesbaei*, honors Mark Catesby (1682–1749), who published the first account of the flora and fauna of North America.

CARDINAL FLOWER
Lobelia cardinalis
Bellflower family (Campanulaceae)
Quick ID: Deep red, tubular flowers line the stalk; the upper "lip" is 2-lobed and the lower lip is 3-lobed; 6" leaves are lance-shaped and toothed.
Height: 24"–48"   **Bloom Season:** July–September

The dramatic velvety red flowers of cardinal flower are outstandingly beautiful showstoppers. The scarlet beauties, native to North and Central America, grow in marshes, open wet meadows, and on streambanks. Most insects find the long tubular flowers too difficult to enter, but the long slender bills of hummingbirds are ideally suited to sip the nectar reward. In the process, the tiny birds pick up pollen on their heads to transport to the next cardinal flower, ensuring pollination. The common name alludes to the bright red robes worn by Roman Catholic cardinals. A great place to see these brilliant flowers is in the wet meadows along Foothills Road at the Blue Ridge Music Center.

FIRE PINK
Silene virginica
Pink family (Caryophyllaceae)
Quick ID: Bright red 1"–1½" star-shaped flowers; 5 narrow, notched petals; sticky, glandular stems and upper leaves; stem leaves opposite and lance-shaped.
Height: 6"–24"   **Bloom Season:** April–August

This showy member of the Pink family of flowers is well named, as the vivid red petals of fire pink steal the show against a backdrop of forest green. The name pink refers to the notched petals of many flowers in this family, just as pinking shears are special scissors that cut in a notched pattern. An alternate name for this plant is scarlet catchfly because these plants are covered with sticky glands that trap small insects attempting to steal the nectar. Rather than insect pollinators, fire pink is pollinated mainly by ruby-throated hummingbirds, which can plunge their long bill into the nectar tube. Look for fire pink in well-drained rocky soil, such as along the Cascades Trail in E. B. Jeffress Park.

PINESAP
Hypopitys monotropa
Heath family (Ericaceae)
Quick ID: Waxy-looking red flowers, usually in clumps, nodding urn-like with pale yellow markings; red soft-hairy stem with flat yellow scale-like leaves.
Height: 4"–10"   **Bloom Season:** July–November

Without the ability to produce chlorophyll, some small flowers such as pinesap must rely on multifaceted relationships for survival. Scientists have discovered that a vast underground network of fungal "roots" called mycelium supports the aboveground life of nearly all plants. When separated from this fungal lifeline, the plants perish. In an intriguing three-way relationship, pinesap derives its existence from a genus of fungus called *Tricholoma* that in turn are interconnected with the roots of trees. In this symbiotic relationship, the trees are supplied with phosphorus and nitrogen from the fungus in exchange for sugars. Currently the pinesap flowers are considered parasites of the fungus, but questions remain to be answered in this complex ecological relationship. In August you may spot these intriguing flowers along the Cascades Trail in E. B. Jeffress Park at Milepost 271.9.

SCARLET BEEBALM
Monarda didyma
Mint family (Lamiaceae)
Quick ID: Clusters of whorled scarlet, tubular flowers; square stem; opposite, serrated, oval leaves.
Height: 30"–60"   **Bloom Season:** July–August

Also known as Oswego tea, scarlet beebalm is a well-known flower along the Parkway. Many native plant gardeners use this beauty to add bright red color to their gardens and to enjoy the hummingbirds that are attracted to the blooms. This eastern native was also well known to early colonists, who used its flavorful leaves as a substitute for imported tea leaves after the 1773 Boston Tea Party event. Colonists also used the leaves in salads and drinks and to flavor jelly. Native Americans used the leaves for many medicinal purposes, including as a balm for bee stings. It also was used to treat flatulence and stomach ailments and to expel worms. Both scarlet beebalm and its relative purple beebalm (*M. fistulosa*) are natural sources of thymol, which is known to kill certain bacteria and fungi.

WILD COLUMBINE
Aquilegia canadensis
Buttercup family (Ranunculaceae)
Quick ID: Nodding red and yellow 1"–2" flowers with 5 upward spurs; numerous yellow protruding stamens; long slender stems; 3-lobed leaflets.

Height: 1'–3'   **Bloom Season:** April–September

With its unusual red backward-pointing spurs, wild columbine does not look much like typical members of the Buttercup family to which it belongs. These 5 spurs hold the sweet nectar reward that is reserved for hummingbirds. Before darting off, the hummingbird unknowingly gathers pollen on its head from the yellow dangling stamens, to be delivered to the next columbine to ensure pollination. Native Americans used an infusion of the plant as a wash for poison ivy and other itches. Some believed that the flower possessed magical powers and could detect bewitchment. Alone in the East, wild columbine has several colorful relatives that live in western states. Look for wild columbine on open rocky slopes and along streambanks along the Blue Ridge Parkway.

INDIAN PAINTBRUSH
Castilleja coccinea
Broomrape family (Orobanchaceae)
Quick ID: Orange-red bracts on dense, hairy stem; small greenish-yellow ¾" flowers with 2 lips; hairy, alternate, lance-shaped leaves.
Height: 8"–20"   **Bloom Season:** April–August

While most species of the colorful members of the paintbrush clan are found in western North America, a few make their homes in the East; one of these is Indian paintbrush, or scarlet paintbrush. The small greenish-yellow flowers are hidden behind eye-catching red bracts that serve to attract hummingbirds. The genus name, *Castilleja*, honors Spanish botanist Domingo Castillejo (1744–1793); and the species name, *coccinea*, is from the Greek word for scarlet. This striking plant is hemiparasitic—its underground roots draw a portion of their water and nutrient supply from other plants, especially grasses. Formerly placed in the Figwort family, Scrophulariaceae, all 200 paintbrush species have been reassigned to the Broomrape family, Orobanchaceae, with other parasitic plants.

81

RED TRILLIUM
Trillium erectum
Trillium family (Trilliaceae)
Quick ID: Flowers with 3 red or white 1"–2⅖" petals; nodding flower heads on stem held above 3 leaves; solid green leaves 2"-8" long and wide; ovary purplish black.
Height: 8"–15"   **Bloom Season:** April–June

Red trillium is common at higher elevations along the Parkway. Like several of the red trilliums, it can also have creamy white petals rather than the normal maroon-red petals. The first week in May is a good time to look for these and other spring blooms along Boone Fork Trail and Green Mountain Overlook. Red trillium goes by many common names, including purple or red purple trillium, erect trillium, wakerobin, or the unflattering "wet dog" trillium. It exudes the musty foul aroma of rotting meat, from which the folk name Stinking Benjamin is derived. *Benjamin* refers to a fragrance used in making incense. Look for red trillium at Craggy Gardens Picnic Area.

SOUTHERN RED TRILLIUM
Trillium sulcatum
Trillium family (Trilliaceae)
Quick ID: Single deep red-maroon or yellowish-white flower, borne on upright 3"–5" stalk held above the leaves, petals with distinctive veins and recurved tips; grooved or keeled sepals tinged with maroon; broad egg-shaped, unmottled, 4"–8" long and wide leaves in whorls of 3.

Height: 12"–24"   **Bloom Season:** April–May

Described by trillium expert Tom Patrick in 1984, southern red trillium has grooves toward the tip of each sepal that help distinguish it from red trillium (*T. erectum*). Also, the flowers of southern red trillium tend to be smaller in diameter than those of red trillium. The species name, *sulcatum*, is in reference to the sulcate sepals, which means having a groove or furrow, as they are keel-shaped somewhat like the tip of a canoe. Southern red trillium often has an earthy smell like that of mushrooms. *Trillium sulcatum* survived the last glacial period by subsisting in warm moist areas of the southern Cumberland Mountains. One of the best places to see this stunning wildflower is along the boardwalk trail at Mabry Mill.

VASEY'S TRILLIUM
Trillium vaseyi
Trillium family (Trilliaceae)
Quick ID: Flowers with 3 maroon or white petals, 2"–5" across, that curve downward at tip; flowers on stem that bends down below the leaves; 3 solid green, broad leaves 4"–8" long and wide with tapering base.
Height: 12"–24"   **Bloom Season:** April–June

Blooming from late April through early June, Vasey's trillium generally blooms later in the growing season than the Parkway's other trilliums. It is most similar to red trillium (*T. erectum*), but the flowers of red trillium sit upward atop their stems while the flower head of Vasey's trillium nods deeply below the leaves. Sometimes called sweet trillium, Vasey's trillium emits a sweet roselike fragrance, while most of the red trilliums stink. One of the largest trilliums, it is named in honor of George Vasey (1822–1893), who was appointed as the US Department of Agriculture's first chief botanist in 1872. A Southern Appalachian endemic, this trillium can be found sporadically in rich coves near the Asheville area and the southernmost part of the Parkway.

BLUE RIDGE PARKWAY TRILLIUM IDENTIFICATION CHART

Species	White (often turn pink)	Red	Flower held below leaves	Distinctive Odor	Leaves with stalk	Leaves without stalk (sessile)	Berry	Anthers	Ovary	Comment
Trillium catesbaei	X		X		X		white	yellow	white	not in VA
Trillium erectum	X	X		foul musty rotting meat		X	maroon	gray to yellowish	dark	high elevations
Trillium grandiflorum	X					X	green	yellow	pale	common
Trillium rugelii	X		X			X	maroon	purple	maroon	not in VA
Trillium simile	X			green apple		X	purple	yellow	dark	not in VA
Trillium sulcatum		X		mushroom		X	maroon	purplish-yellow	dark purple	mid-elevations
Trillium undulatum	X				X		red	reddish-white	white	acidic habitats
Trillium vaseyi		X	X	rosy sweet			maroon	grayish-purple	maroon	not in VA

BUTTERFLY WEED
Asclepias tuberosa
Dogbane family (Apocynaceae)
Quick ID: Bright orange clustered flowers with 5 reflexed petals; alternate, oblong, pointed 2"–4" leaves; clear rather than milky sap; fruits are dry, brown, elongated pods that split, releasing silky tufts attached to seeds.
Height: 1'–2'   **Bloom Season:** June–August

Not a subtle orange, perhaps a better descriptive of the color of butterfly weed is clown orange, making this flower one of the easiest to identify. Sometimes called butterfly milkweed, the striking orange petals act as butterfly magnets, summoning such species as monarchs, fritillaries, and swallowtails. Ruby-throated hummingbirds also sip the sweet nectar. The genus name, *Asclepias*, honors Asclepius, the Greek god of healing. It is sometimes called pleurisy root, as Native Americans used the root as a cure for pleurisy and other lung ailments. Recently scientists have found that it contains a cardiac glycoside, which is a chemical that affects the heart and other body systems. This is the active ingredient in some heart medications but can be poisonous in large doses.

SPOTTED JEWELWEED
Impatiens capensis
Touch-me-not family (Balsaminaceae)

Quick ID: Orange 1" flowers with forward-curving spur, 2 lower rounded petals with cone-shaped flower body; flowers hang in thin stem; alternate, oval, coarsely toothed 1"–4" leaves; tall smooth succulent stems.

Height: 2'–5'   **Bloom Season:** July–September

In late summer, large stands of the bright orange flowers of spotted jewelweed are magnets for ruby-throated hummingbirds, which energetically defend their territory. Another name for this plant is spotted touch-me-not, as the slightest touch will make the mature seedpods pop with explosive action, flinging the seeds up to 5' away. Sap of the stems and leaves has long been used as a folk treatment to calm the itch from poison ivy and stinging nettles. Jewelweed contains chemical components called saponins that break down the urushiol responsible for the contact dermatitis caused by exposure to poison ivy. Recent studies have shown the chemicals in jewelweed may be effective against some breast and colon cancers. The related pale touch-me-not (*I. pallida*) has yellow flowers.

FLAME AZALEA
Rhododendron calendulaceum
Heath family (Ericaceae)
Quick ID: Shrub; orange funnel-shaped flowers with 5 spreading lobes; 1"–3" long oval leaves.

Height: 6'–10'   **Bloom Season:** April–July

One of the most spectacular of all native shrubs, the bright orange blooms of flame azalea stand ablaze against the green forest foliage. From a distance the color is so intense that it appears that there are fires burning on far hillsides. Even though they lack any sweet odor, these shrubs attract bees, butterflies, and hummingbirds with their bright color. The stamens of the flower protrude in long arching projections eager to brush pollen on these visitors. At lower elevations the flowering time varies from April to May and into June, depending on the elevation, and the blooming period may continue into July at higher elevations. Do not be tempted to pick these or any other flowers—it is illegal along the Parkway—but you can see them at Whetstone Ridge and Craggy Gardens Visitor Center.

ORANGE DAYLILY
Hemerocallis fulva
Daylily family (Hemerocallidaceae)
Quick ID: Large orange lily-like flowers, usually with dark spots or stripes, in clusters of 5–9; flexible, round, leafless stem; long 1'–3' strap-like leaves.
Height: 2'–4'   **Bloom Season:** May–July

Wildflower purists may not appreciate the orange daylily, or tiger lily, as it is an introduced species that sometimes escapes cultivation and finds its way into the wild. Early settlers to the region often planted the large orange flowers, as the showy plant spread easily and covered bare ground with long leaves and bright color. Unfortunately, once daylilies have become established, they spread from thick underground tubers and quickly overtake native plants. This native of East Asia is sometimes confused with other orange flowers, including Canada lily (*Lilium canadense*) and Turk's cap lily (*L. superbum*). Rather than being placed in the Lily family, Liliaceae, orange daylily has a family of its own called Hemerocallidaceae or sometimes Xanthorrhoeaceae.

GRAY'S LILY
Lilium grayi
Lily family (Liliaceae)
Quick ID: 6 deep reddish-orange bell-shaped flowers with dark spots inside the petals, yellowish-orange throat; pointed 4" leaves in whorls of 4–8.
Height: 2'–4'   **Bloom season:** June–July

Appalachian endemic flowers make their home in these rolling mountains and nowhere else on Earth. Gray's lily is one such flower, found only in a few specialized habitats in Virginia, North Carolina, and Tennessee. Found in grassy balds and wet meadows, this lovely lily honors Asa Gray (1810–1888), the nineteenth-century botanist whose *Gray's Manual of Botany* was the leading textbook for field naturalists for many years. With such a restricted range and relatively few populations, Gray's lily is a plant that needs our help to preserve and protect it. Habitat destruction, illegal collecting, and overgrazing by herbivores are threats to this special lily, which is protected within the boundaries of the Blue Ridge Parkway.

CAROLINA LILY
Lilium michauxii
Lily family (Liliaceae)

Quick ID: 6 orange petals strongly curved backward, throat becoming yellow with brownish-purple spots, protruding stamens; pointed 2½"–5" leaves in whorls of 3–7, becoming smaller as they go up the stem.

Height: 2'–4'   **Bloom Season:** June–August

In 2003 Carolina lily was designated the state wildflower of North Carolina. Carolina lily prefers dry areas unlike other lilies along the Parkway, including Turk's cap lily (*L. superbum*), which thrives in moist areas. Turk's cap lily is also taller than Carolina lily. The Latin name of this lily honors influential botanist André Michaux (1746–1802), who made significant contributions to the early study of the plants of the United States and Canada. Butterflies such as eastern tiger swallowtails pollinate the fragrant flowers.

TURK'S CAP LILY

Lilium superbum
Lily family (Liliaceae)
Quick ID: Several large orange, drooping flowers with spotted reddish-brown recurved petals; tall, flexible stem; lance-shaped leaves in whorls.
Height: 3'–7'
Bloom Season: July–August

Popping out 8 to 10 graceful flowers on each plant, Turk's cap lily can look like decorations for a party. Stretching up to 7' tall, this is the tallest member of the Lily family found along the Parkway. The petals of this lily are strongly recurved, which helps to identify it from the other orange lilies found here. The common name Turk's cap comes from the flower's similarity to a colorful traditional Turkish felt hat with recurved brim and pointed top. The typically redder petals of Canada lilies (*L. canadense*) (inset) are not as recurved as those of Turk's cap lily. The rare Gray's lily (*L. grayi*) has redder petals; Michaux's or Carolina lily (*L. michauxii*) is typically lighter orange with broader leaves.

YELLOW FRINGED ORCHID
Platanthera ciliaris
Orchid family (Orchidaceae)

Quick ID: Orange or bright yellow 1½" flowers at top of stalk, lower petal finely fringed, 3 petal-like sepals and 2 lateral petals, long drooping spur at back of flower; alternate, 2"–8" long leaves are lance shaped and keeled.

Height: 12"–36"   **Bloom Season:** July–August

With its brilliant orange or bright yellow flowers, yellow fringed orchid is one of the showiest members of the Orchid family. The species name, *ciliaris*, means "fringed," and just like snowflakes, no two flowers have the exact same fringe pattern. In our area, the petals are usually orange rather than yellow, begging the alternate name of orange fringed orchid. Found in sunny but moist areas, the plants may not bloom if conditions are not optimal. Butterflies such as fritillaries and swallowtails are attracted to the intricately fringed petals. This orchid's spectacular beauty may be its own worst enemy—its populations are being reduced due to unethical (and illegal) plant collection along the Parkway. Please leave these and all other wildflowers for others to enjoy.

LARGE-FLOWERED BELLWORT
Uvularia grandiflora
Peruvian Lily family (Alstroemeriaceae)
Quick ID: Golden-yellow, narrow, drooping flowers with 6 twisted, overlapping 1"–2" long petals; alternate leaves encircle the stem (perfoliate).
Height: 15"–30" **Bloom Season:** April–May

The 6 narrow golden-yellow petals of large-flowered bellwort are overlapping and twisted like when a worried child winds its hair. Like large-flowered bellwort, the stem of perfoliate bellwort (*U. perfoliata*) also passes through the leaves, but its pale yellow petals aren't twisted. The stems of mountain or Appalachian bellwort (*U. pudica*) (inset) and wild oats (*U. sessilifolia*) do not pass through the leaves. The thin bell-shaped flowers were thought to resemble the uvula that hangs down from the soft palate in the throat, hence the genus name, *Uvularia*. Native Americans taught early colonists to eat the young, tender bellwort stems like asparagus. The mashed root was steeped into tea for diarrhea, and a poultice was made to treat boils.

GOLDEN ALEXANDERS
Zizia aurea
Carrot family (Apiaceae)
Quick ID: 2" flat-topped yellow flowers, 10 small stalks with a cluster of tiny flowers, central flower without stalk; alternate leaves, finely toothed leaflets.
Height: 1'–3'   **Bloom Season:** April–June

The flat-topped yellow head of golden Alexanders looks somewhat like a flattened umbrella. This type of flower head is called an umbel, from the Latin word for parasol. These flowers were named golden Alexanders, alluding to the "golden age" of Alexander the Great. The genus, *Zizia*, honors German botanist Johann Baptist Ziz (1779–1820). The species name, *aurea*, comes from the Latin word for "golden yellow." Golden Alexanders is often confused with several other similar flowers, including heart-leaved meadow parsnip (*Z. aptera*), which has heart-shaped basal leaves, and yellow pimpernel (*Taenidia integerrima*), which has untoothed leaflets. Black swallowtail butterflies lay their eggs on these plants; when hatched, the caterpillars eat the sharp-toothed leaves and flowers.

GREEN AND GOLD

Chrysogonum virginianum
Aster family (Asteraceae)

Quick ID: Short, single golden flowers, 5 rounded rays, yellow central disk; 1"–3" opposite leaves strongly veined, oval to spade-shaped, hairy and shallowly toothed; long stalks.

Height: 2"–12"   **Bloom Season:** March–June

Found in open woods and along forest edges, green and gold is a small plant with bright golden petals and dark green leaves. Many yellow asters are difficult to identify, but few have only 5 petals (ray flowers). Another good clue is the hairy, deeply veined leaves. Look for green and golds at Humpback Rocks Visitor Center. Blooming much later in the year (June–October), another yellow aster, Maryland golden-aster (*Chrysopsis mariana*) (insets), has a 1'–2' silky stem, with alternate leaves on the stem. Golden-asters are sometimes called silkgrass due to their silky, hairy stems. The 1" yellow daisy-like flowers with yellow centers bloom in clumps. They are often found in well-drained soils, such as near the Blue Ridge Parkway Visitor Center in Asheville.

STAR TICKSEED
Coreopsis pubescens
Aster family (Asteraceae)
Quick ID: Bright yellow daisy-like flowers, 2" wide, 8 yellow rays, petal tips notched; 2 opposite leaves, usually hairy.
Height: 20'–40'   **Bloom Season:** July–September

At least 7 species of coreopsis can be found along the Blue Ridge Parkway. Star tickseed has distinctively notched tips on the petals that give it a starry appearance. The leaves of another tickseed, woodland or greater tickseed (*C. major*) (top inset) are very distinctive. Even though it appears that there are 6 leaves, there are actually only 2 leaves that are deeply cut and seem to form a whorl around the stem. Woodland coreopsis can be found at Heintooga Road, Mount Mitchell State Park, and Flat Rock Trail. Whorled or threadleaf tickseed (*C. verticillata*) (bottom inset), which blooms in early summer, has extremely narrow whorled leaves and can be found in dry woodlands and forest edges, especially in the northern section of the Parkway.

ROUGHLEAF SUNFLOWER

Helianthus strumosus
Aster family (Asteraceae)

Quick ID: Bright yellow flowers, 2½"–3½" wide, on very tall branching stems, 9–15 ray petals; mostly opposite 3"–8" leaves, shallowly toothed and broadly lance-shaped, rough on the top side, pale and somewhat hairy under the leaf; smooth, whitish stem.

Height: 3'–7'   **Bloom Season:** July–September

More than 10 species of sunflower have been found along the Parkway, and many are challenging to identify. One common species is called roughleaf sunflower; the leaves are rough on the top and a bit hairy and pale whitish underneath. A similar flower called Jerusalem artichoke (*H. tuberosus*) (inset), which is neither an artichoke nor from Jerusalem, was cultivated by Native Americans as a nutritious food. Unlike the smooth stems of roughleaf sunflower, the flower stalks of Jerusalem artichoke are rough, and it has large sandpapery leaves. The underground tubers have a flavor not unlike artichokes and are used like potatoes, but as they tend to cause flatulence, they were often used for livestock. High in folate, the nutritious seeds of sunflowers are helpful during pregnancy to prevent birth defects.

MOUNTAIN DWARF DANDELION
Krigia montana
Aster family (Asteraceae)

Quick ID: Single bright yellow dandelion-like flower growing in clumps, yellow ray petals squared at the end and sharply notched; leafless stalks; linear leaves that may be coarsely toothed near the base.

Height: 4"–15"   **Bloom Season:** May–September

Not all dandelions are the familiar flower that grows in our yards. Mountain dwarf dandelion, or mountain Cynthia, is a special Southern Appalachian endemic that grows at high elevations in very specific habitats, such as moist cliffs and along rocky mountain streambanks. An introduced species that looks something like mountain dwarf dandelion is spotted cat's ear (*Hypochaeris radicata*). The leaves are covered in firm coarse hairs that look like spots. Mount Pisgah picnic grounds parking area is a great place to see spotted cat's ear, which sometimes cover the ground in a sheet of yellow.

GOLDEN RAGWORT
Packera aurea
Aster family (Asteraceae)
Quick ID: Flat-topped clusters of ¾" daisy-like yellow flowers with 8–12 rays; 1"–6" heart-shaped basal leaves with blunt teeth and long stalks; stem leaves, lobed, pointed.
Height: 12"–30" **Bloom Season:** March–June

An unusually named flower, ragworts are members of the large Aster family. Golden ragwort tends to grow in moist areas along the Blue Ridge Parkway. The 2 very differently shaped types of leaves are characteristic of golden ragwort. The bottom or basal leaves are heart-shaped with small blunt teeth; the upper leaves are long, divided into many lobes, and have large teeth at the ends. It is the highly cut leaves that give this plant a raggedy appearance, hence the name ragwort. *Wort* is an Old English word (*wyrt*) meaning "plant." Blooming a bit later, the similar flowered Appalachian or Small's ragwort (*P. anonyma*) (bottom inset) has elongated basal leaves. The ragworts have recently undergone a genus change from *Senecio* to *Packera* and may be listed as the former in older references.

YELLOW HAWKWEED
Pilosella caespitosa
Aster family (Asteraceae)

Quick ID: Small yellow flowers on clusters at top of wiry stem, flat flower heads about ½" wide; stems have black glandular hairs; oval to lance-shaped basal leaves are softly hairy on both sides.

Height: 10"–36"   **Bloom Season:** May–October

Sometimes called yellow king-devil, yellow hawkweed is an introduced species native to Europe. Due to recent molecular findings, the taxonomic name has been changed from *Hieracium caespitosum* or *H. pretense* to *Pilosella caespitosa*. Yellow hawkweed is one of the common yellow flowers found along the roadside. The leaves of a similar flower called rattlesnake weed (*Hieracium venosum*) (top inset) are strongly purple veined, somewhat resembling the markings on a rattlesnake. A smaller plant, mouse-eared hawkweed (*P. officinarum*) (bottom inset), blooms May–July. These yellow dandelion-like flowers are only about 8" tall but have silvery-gray leaves that feel like felt. Mouse-eared hawkweed contains a compound that acts as a blood thinner. It also has antibiotic properties that act against brucellosis, which infects cattle and sometimes humans.

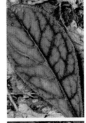

BLACK-EYED SUSAN
Rudbeckia hirta
Aster family (Asteraceae)
Quick ID: 10–20 bright yellow ray flowers 2"–4" across, dark blackish-brown center; alternate lance to oval bristly, hairy leaves; bristly, hairy stem
Height: 1'–3' **Bloom Season:** June–October

The familiar yellow black-eyed Susans adorn roadsides and meadows in summer. No one is sure how this flower got its name, but legend says it comes from an Old English poem written by John Gay (1685–1732). In the poem, Susan, who had black eyes, boarded a ship to search for her beloved, sweet William (alluding to the flower called sweet William, *Dianthus barbatus*) to wish him protection from harm before he set sail. The bushier brown-eyed Susan, or thinleaf coneflower (*R. triloba*), has smaller flower heads than black-eyed Susan and has fewer yellow ray flowers. Two Southern Appalachian endemic varieties of brown-eyed Susans can be found along the Parkway: Chauncey's coneflower (*R. triloba* var. *beadlei*) and Blue Ridge three-lobed coneflower (*R. triloba* var. *rupestris*).

GREEN-HEADED CONEFLOWER
Rudbeckia laciniata
Aster family (Asteraceae)

Quick ID: Tall yellow, branching sunflower-like; 6–16 yellow drooping petals (ray flowers), greenish-yellow center disk; smooth stems often whitish; alternate leaves divided into 3–7 sharply pointed lobes.

Height: 3'–9'   **Bloom Season:** July–October

In the same genus as the familiar black-eyed Susan, green-headed or cut-leaf coneflowers are very tall sunflower-like plants with yellow petals. In moist forests at high elevations in the northern portion of the Southern Appalachians, a variety called Blue Ridge cutleaf coneflower (*R. laciniata* var. *humilis*) has leaves that are usually 3-lobed as opposed to the typical 5 lobes of other green-headed coneflowers. Like a short, bushy, green-headed coneflower, brown-eyed Susan, or thinleaf coneflower (*R. triloba*), also has leaves with 3 lobes but is much shorter, standing 2'–5'. Instead of a greenish flower center, the flowers of brown-eyed Susan are brownish-black. Native Americans gathered the young leaves and stems and cooked them as greens or hung them in the sun to dry for later use.

TALL GOLDENROD
Solidago altissima
Aster family (Asteraceae)

Quick ID: Tall masses of tiny yellow flowers arranged along upper side of stems; downy, rigid stem; alternate 3"–6" leaves, 3 main veins, underside hairy.

Height: 1½'–6½'   **Bloom Season:** August–October

The feathery plumes of tall goldenrod are a sure sign that autumn has arrived. Very common throughout the Parkway, it is found in most parts of North America except for a few western states and provinces. The plant produces chemicals that suppress the growth of other plants. Growing from underground rhizomes, it forms colonies of clones with identical DNA. In response to stem-boring insects, galls often form on goldenrods, including pretty rosettes at the top of stems. Two species of goldenrod are very similar to the abundant tall goldenrod. Less common in the park, Canada goldenrod (*S. canadensis*) has sharply toothed leaves with hairs on the underside veins. Smooth goldenrod (*S. gigantea*) grows in wet meadows has tiny serrations on the smooth leaves.

CURTIS'S APPALACHIAN GOLDENROD
Solidago curtisii
Aster family (Asteraceae)

Quick ID: Clusters of yellow flowers at leaf bases; erect angled stem finely grooved; serrated narrow, lance-shaped leaves with tapered tip.

Height: 2'–3' **Bloom Season:** August-October

Along with tall goldenrod, this is one of the most common goldenrods found along the Parkway. Instead of the sunny meadows where most other goldenrods bloom, you are more likely to find Curtis's Appalachian goldenrod along trails in shaded deciduous forests. The species name, *curtisii*, honors botanist Moses Ashley Curtis (1808–1872), who explored the southern Appalachian Mountains collecting specimens of plants, lichens, and fungi. Humpback Rocks Picnic Area is a great place to pack a picnic lunch and see a variety of goldenrods. Here under a shady canopy of hickories and oaks you can find several species of goldenrod, including Curtis's Appalachian. Another very common species in the park, sharp-leaved goldenrod (*S. arguta*), is also found here, as are the whitish flowers of silverrod (*S. bicolor*).

105

SKUNK GOLDENROD
Solidago glomerata
Aster family (Asteraceae)
Quick ID: Relatively large, dense, rounded yellow flower heads; leaves serrated 4"–10".
Height: 1'–4'   **Bloom Season:** July–October

A Southern Appalachian endemic restricted to North Carolina and Tennessee, skunk goldenrod grows at high elevations in the park. It is commonly seen on rocky outcrops, on heath balds, and in spruce-fir forests.

Even though goldenrods do not cause hay fever and allergies, you may not want to stick your nose in this flower—its odor has an uncanny likeness to that of a skunk. The pollen of goldenrods is heavy and thick and can't be carried on the wind. But they bloom at the same time as ragweed (*Ambrosia* spp.), which *does* cause many allergy sufferers to sniffle and sneeze. Just off the Parkway, another high-altitude lover, Blue Ridge goldenrod (*S. spithamaea*) (bottom inset) grows on nearby Grandfather Mountain.

ROAN MOUNTAIN GOLDENROD
Solidago roanensis
Aster family (Asteraceae)
Quick ID: Yellow flowers clustered at top of stem; upright hairy, reddish stem; alternate 2"–6" leaves oblong to diamond sharply toothed.
Height: 8"–39"   **Bloom Season:** July–September

About 20 species of goldenrod can be found within Parkway boundaries, along with another 17 varieties or subspecies. First collected on nearby Roan Mountain on the North Carolina–Tennessee border, Roan Mountain goldenrod can be found in mountainous regions from Pennsylvania to Georgia. Its slender wand-like clusters of bright yellow flowers prefer well-drained soils in open, rocky areas with lots of sunlight. Another species that can be found along the Parkway is downy goldenrod (*S. puberula*) (top right), which has small hairs on the stem and narrower leaves. With flowers tightly appressed to the single upright stem, silverrod, or white goldenrod (*S. bicolor*) (bottom right), is the yellowish-white color of shoepeg corn.

107

COMMON DANDELION
Taraxacum officinale
Aster family (Asteraceae)

Quick ID: Slightly rounded yellow flowers on single stem, numerous yellow rays; hollow stem with milky sap; leaves 2"–10", deeply and irregularly toothed lobes.

Height: 2"–18"   **Bloom Season:** March–October

One of the most widely recognized of all wildflowers, the common dandelion may also be the most despised of all plants. Millions of dollars are spent each year to poison and kill this pugnacious plant. Considered a weed, the dandelion has evolved to be one of the most successful wildflowers ever known. After a long winter, settlers relished the fresh greens as a welcome and healthful addition to meals, used in salads or cooked. Dandelions boast more vitamin A than carrots. They also contain more vitamin C, iron, and calcium than spinach. The flower petals were traditionally made into a delicate wine. The serrated or toothed appearance of the leaves, which resemble a lion's teeth, gave rise to the plant's name—in French, *dent de lion*.

WINGSTEM
Verbesina alternifolia
Aster family (Asteraceae)
Quick ID: Masses of lazy yellow 1" flowers, 2–10 petals (ray flowers) irregularly spaced and bent backward (reflexed), prominent center with yellow disk flowers forming a sphere; leaves primarily alternate (the lowermost sometimes opposite), narrow, lance-shaped, serrated; stem has fleshy raised keels or wings.

Height: 3'–10'   **Bloom Season:** July–September

The tall daisy-like yellow flowers of wingstem look untidy, as they tend to droop backward on the flower head. The stem between the leaves has noticeable fleshy ridges, or wings, that are characteristic and help to distinguish this plant from true sunflowers. Crownbeard, or stickseed (*V. occidentalis*) (right), is very similar to wingstem, but if you look carefully at the leaf arrangement on the stem, the leaves are opposite each other rather than the alternately placed leaves of wingstem. The yellow petals (ray flowers) of crownbeard tend to be less reflexed than those of wingstem. With a casual glance, sneezeweed (*Helenium autumnale*), a yellow flower found in wetlands , seems similar, but the yellow flower petals (rays) are fan-shaped. Purplehead sneezeweed (*H. flexuosum*) has a purple center.

PALE JEWELWEED
Impatiens pallida
Touch-me-not family (Balsaminaceae)
Quick ID: Pale yellow 1"–1½" flowers, cone-shaped with spur held at right angle, 2 lower rounded petals; flowers hang on thin stems; alternate, oval, serrated 4" leaves; tall, smooth, succulent stems.
Height: 3'–6'   **Bloom Season:** July–September

The hood-shaped yellow flowers of pale jewelweed, or touch-me-not, nod like a child's yoyo in passing breezes. Pale jewelweed and its cousin, spotted jewelweed (*I. capensis*), can be found in moist areas along the Parkway. Native Americans used the clear watery sap of both these plants as a salve for skin irritations. Early settlers learned to use these native plants in similar ways. The sap was used to remove warts, treat ringworm, and cleanse skin ulcers. Settlers also used it as a remedy for jaundice and gave it as a drink to patients with dropsy, an old-fashioned term for edema or swelling. As long as pale jewelweed is somewhat sheltered from the sun, it can withstand a bit drier conditions than spotted jewelweed.

MOUNTAIN ST. JOHN'S WORT
Hypericum graveolens
St. John's Wort family (Hypericaceae)
Quick ID: 5 yellow petals, usually without black spots, numerous protruding stamens; usually unbranched stems; opposite rounded to oval 1" wide leaves, black spots.
Height: 12"–23"   **Bloom Season:** July–August

While common St. John's wort (*H. perforatum*) can be found in many habitats, several species of Southern Appalachian endemic St. John's wort only grow at high elevations. Mountain St. John's wort only grows at the highest elevations in the Appalachians, generally above 3,900' or more. Blue Ridge St. John's wort (*H. mitchellianum*) can be found growing in grassy balds and seepage areas at moderate to high elevations above 3,200'. Granite dome St. John's wort (*H. buckleyi*) is a very short, mat-forming plant that rarely reaches above 12" in height. The limited distribution of these plants adds to the importance of conservation efforts to prevent losing these rare species to habitat loss and other threats.

COMMON ST. JOHN'S WORT
Hypericum perforatum
St. John's Wort family (Hypericaceae)
Quick ID: Bright yellow flowers, black dots on the 5 petal margins, numerous protruding stamens; branched woody stems; opposite linear leaves with translucent dots.
Height: 12"–30" **Bloom Season:** June–September

The medicinal use of the bright yellow, starry flowers of St. John's wort dates back to the ancient Greek healer Hippocrates. This flower blooms close to the birthday of John the Baptist (June 24), whom the name honors. It was gathered for use as a dye or medicine, or to be hung in the doorway to keep evil spirits and witches from entering the home. Today there is some scientific evidence that St. John's wort may be useful for mild depression. Unfortunately, side effects are numerous. It can cause negative interactions with such medications as birth control pills, antidepressants, heart medications, anticoagulants, and some cancer medications. First brought to North America by settlers in 1696, more than 12 species can be found along the Blue Ridge Parkway.

BLUEBEAD LILY
Clintonia borealis
Lily family (Liliaceae)

Quick ID: 3–8 greenish-yellow, nodding bell-shaped flowers, 6 petals (3 petals, 3 sepals) with yellow stamens that protrude; 2–5 glossy green 4"–16" leaves with conspicuous, depressed mid-vein; fruits are bright blue oval berries.

Height: 6"–16" **Bloom Season:** May–June

The high altitude spruce-fir forests of the Blue Ridge Parkway are where you can find bluebead lily. Also called yellow Clintonia, or simply Clintonia, the plant is a member of the Lily family characterized by leaves with parallel veins. The Latin name, *Clintonia*, was given to honor DeWitt Clinton, governor of New York from 1769 to 1828, who wrote books on natural history. The species name, *borealis*, means it is considered a northern inhabitant. The common name bluebead comes from the midnight-blue rounded to oval berries that replace the 6-petaled yellowish-green flowers in the fall. Very slow growing, it may take 10–12 years for this plant to flower.

TROUT LILY
Erythronium umbilicatum
Lily family (Liliaceae)

Quick ID: 1 yellow nodding flower, 6 recurved petals with bronzy markings on the back of the petals, 6 yellow-brown stamens protrude; 2 opposite 4"-8" elliptical leaves, mottled with purple and brown.

Height: 6"–9" **Bloom Season:** February–April

An early-spring hike along Parkway trails may delight hikers with the yellow nodding flowers of trout lily. Trout lilies are so named because the leaves are mottled with brownish-gray markings that are similar to those of a trout. One of the earliest blooming spring wildflowers, trout lilies have a very short growing season; by the time the surrounding trees get their leaves, the plant has started to fade away. Look for colonies of trout lilies in February or early April along Boone Fork Trail. At higher elevations you may find this and other early-spring wildflowers blooming later in the season. A high-altitude variety, Southern Appalachian trout lily (*E. umbilicatum* var. *monostolum*), is an Appalachian endemic.

INDIAN CUCUMBER ROOT
Medeola virginiana
Lily family (Liliaceae)

Quick ID: Pale yellow to greenish-yellow flowers that hang downward beneath the top whorl of leaves; tapered, elliptic leaves in 1 or 2 whorls on the wiry stem; fruit dark purple-black berries.

Height: 12"–30"   **Bloom Season:** April–June

Hiding beneath 2 tiers of whorled leaves, the small greenish-yellow flowers of Indian cucumber root are a bit difficult to spot. When the dark purplish berries appear in fall, they rise to the top of the leaves to attract animals and birds, which will spread the seeds. Native to eastern North America, Indian cucumber root is found scattered in rich woods throughout the Parkway. The common name refers to the flavor of the root, called a rhizome, which has a brittle texture and tastes a bit like cucumbers. The genus name, *Medeola*, is derived from a mythical Greek sorceress called Medea, who used magic herbs and potions to exact her will on others. Look for this plant along trails such as Cascades, Flat Rock, and Linville Falls.

115

DAFFODIL
Narcissus pseudonarcissus
Amaryllis family (Amaryllidaceae)
Quick ID: Yellow petals fused into an open trumpet-shaped tube, 6 yellow petal-like structures (tepals) surround trumpet; 1–10 flowers per plant; leaves flattened and grooved.
Height: 6"–12"   **Bloom Season:** March–April

Although cultivated plants, including daffodils, have entertained horticulturists for centuries, they are not considered native wildflowers to Virginia or North Carolina. Nevertheless, when early settlers reached the Blue Ridge Mountains, they planted many seeds and bulbs from familiar European plants. Commonly called daffodil, jonquil, or narcissus, these long-lived descendants can be seen blooming at old homesites and graveyards along the Parkway. In Greek mythology, Narcissus was so enthralled with his own beauty that he died staring into a pool at his own reflection, leaving only the flower as remembrance. Even though all parts of daffodils are poisonous, a drug called galantamine has been derived from daffodils and is currently used to inhibit the memory loss associated with Alzheimer's disease.

YELLOW MANDARIN
Prosartes lanuginosa
Lily family (Liliaceae)

Quick ID: Greenish-yellow bell or star-shaped flowers; 6 narrow, sharply pointed petals; flowers dangle singly or in pairs from crooked stem; downy leaves with prominent veins; fruit reddish-orange berries.

Height: 18"–30"   **Bloom Season:** April–June

The delicate flowers of yellow mandarin quiver silently with the slightest breeze that passes through shaded forests along the Blue Ridge Parkway. Occurring in pairs at the ends of forked branches, the greenish-yellow bell-shaped flowers dangle partially hidden beneath the leaves. The common name yellow fairybells describes the delicate hanging flowers. Formerly in the genus *Disporum*, yellow mandarin is actually related to rosy twisted stalk (*Streptopus lanceolatus*) and therefore is now placed in the genus *Prosartes*. Rosy twisted stalk has single nodding pink flowers hanging from each leaf axil along the stem. Yellow mandarin is found in the unglaciated Appalachians and the Ozark Mountains of Arkansas. Look for yellow mandarin in rich woods, such as those the Boone Fork Trail passes through.

SUNDROPS
Oenothera fruticosa
Evening Primrose family (Onagraceae)
Quick ID: 1" flowers with 4 bright yellow petals that are notched at the end, 8 orange stamens; alternate, lance-shaped 2½" leaves.
Height: 12"–36"   **Bloom Season:** April–August

Blooming through much of the summer, the bright yellow flowers of sundrops are one of the most common wildflowers along the Parkway. Found in open areas, sundrops quickly colonizes areas with poor soil and is relatively drought tolerant. Widespread in eastern North America, there are at least 7 species of *Oenothera* found along the Parkway. Evening primrose (*O. biennis*), a look-alike, only starts to bloom at dusk and is pollinated mainly by hawk moths. Sundrops is pollinated mostly by bees. In fall the seeds of sundrops are eaten by birds. Native Americans ate the young leaves; the roots were heated, mashed, and made into a poultice for inflamed hemorrhoids.

PUTTYROOT

Aplectrum hyemale
Orchid family (Orchidaceae)

Quick ID: Yellowish-green to brown flowers with purple tips, ¾"–1" hooded, nodding; single leaf, purplish on the underside, withers away before the flower blooms.

Height: 10"–16"　　　　　　　　　　　　**Bloom Season:** May–June

Growing in rich dappled woods, the flowers of puttyroot are difficult to see against the brown leaf litter. Like crane-fly orchid (*Tipularia discolor*), the leaves of puttyroot flowers are present during winter but then wither away before the flower appears. Although similar, the leaves of puttyroot are narrow and elliptic and folded along the veins, while those of crane-fly orchid are ovate and not folded. The yellowish-brown flower has been described as sallow or dingy, but if you look closely, it is quite a beauty. The underground bulbs, called corms, are attached by a slender thread, leading to another common name, Adam and Eve. Early settlers obtained a mucilaginous substance from the corms that was used to repair pottery.

119

YELLOW LADY'S SLIPPER
Cypripedium parviflorum
Orchid family (Orchidaceae)
Quick ID: Yellow, inflated 2" pouch-shaped flower, 2 spirally twisted petals; alternate 3"–8" leaves that are pleated, hairy, elliptical.

Height: 8"–28"   **Bloom Season:** April–June

No other flower evokes more passion and compelling allure than an orchid. The lady's slipper, or moccasin flower, is one of at least 30 orchid species recorded within the boundaries of the Blue Ridge Parkway. Both yellow and pink lady slippers (*C. acaule*) are found here. Lady's slippers have a balloon-like pouch that resembles the bedroom slipper of an elf. In Latin the species name means "a little shoe." Lady's slipper orchids have evolved a hinged lip that acts like an insect trap. The edges of the large pouch are curled inward, prohibiting the insect from backing out. Instead, it must exit through one of the small openings at the back of the flower; in doing so it picks up pollen to be carried to the next flower.

APPALACHIAN FALSE FOXGLOVE
Aureolaria levigata
Broomrape family (Orobanchaceae)
Quick ID: Yellow funnel-shaped flowers on smooth stem, flowers about 1" long, 5 flaring petals; opposite 1½"–4" lance-shaped leaves.

Height: 2'–5'   **Bloom Season:** August–September

The funnel-shaped flowers of Appalachian false foxglove flare like the end of a trumpet. An alternate name for this flower is Appalachian oak leach, as members of this genus are semi-parasitic on the roots of oaks. Yellow false foxglove (*A. flava*) is similar but has purplish stems. Growing in disturbed areas, an introduced plant called butter-and-eggs (*Linaria vulgaris*) has spread across North America. The bright yellow flowers also sit atop a stem, but the flowers have a long spur and the lower lip has orange on it. Another common name is toadflax, as the leaves are similar to those of flax and the flower can be pressed to imitate the opening and closing mouth of a croaking frog.

121

SQUAWROOT
Conopholis americana
Broomrape family (Orobanchaceae)
Quick ID: 1" thick, erect, yellow-brown stem from ground; tiny whitish-yellow flowers; scaly leaf-like appendages.
Height: 2"–8"   **Bloom Season:** April–June

Passing through rich, leaf-strewn forests, hikers tell tales of a small, mysterious object growing up through the leaf litter along trails. When trying to describe it, they use terms such as "yellowish-brown," "corncob," and "fleshy pinecone" sticking up from the ground. They think this curious object is a plant, but they are not sure. This surprising little plant is indeed a wildflower, but one that does not produce chlorophyll and therefore never turns green. The underground roots are parasitic on oak roots, forming a gall from which the flower emerges years later. Commonly called squawroot, it was collected by Native Americans as a food source. It is also a major food source for black bears, composing up to 40 percent of their annual diet.

BEECHDROPS
Epifagus virginiana
Broomrape family (Orobanchaceae)

Quick ID: Inconspicuous, thin, creamy tan stems; inconspicuous whitish flowers streaked with purplish to brown stripes occur singly on stems; alternate scaly leaves.

Height: 6"–18"   **Bloom Season:** August–November

Considered hiccups of the plant kingdom, parasitic plants do not contain chlorophyll and therefore are unable to make their own food. One such parasitic plant, beechdrops, depends on the American beech (*Fagus grandifolia*), a long-lived tree of eastern forests. Reliant on securing nourishment from these trees, beechdrops insert a rootlike structure into a beech root and in autumn send up inconspicuous stems with tiny flowers. Resembling dying stems, beechdrops are widespread in the East, but it takes some botanical sleuthing to locate this plant—from a distance they look brownish and blend in amazingly well with the surrounding leaf layer. Look for beechdrops along the Trail of Trees at the James River Visitor Center.

LOUSEWORT
Pedicularis canadensis
Broomrape family (Orobanchaceae)

Quick ID: Yellow flowers mixed with reddish-purple on thick stem; tubular flowers with a hood encircle stem; leaflike bracts; leaves soft-hairy, basal or stem leaves alternate, deeply divided and fernlike; often forms low-growing colonies.

Height: 5"–14"   **Bloom Season:** April–June

The encircling flowers of lousewort, or wood betony, can be yellow, reddish, or a combination of both colors. This widespread plant is commonly called lousewort from the belief that cattle and sheep that grazed on this plant would become infested with lice. Particularly well adapted to survive in stressful situations, lousewort is partially parasitic on other plants and forms a mycorrhizal relationship with certain fungi. The Cherokee called this plant "owl head," as it somewhat resembles the wet feathers of an owl after a rainy night. They made a hot "tea" from the roots to treat stomachaches or diarrhea. The roots were also steeped and made into a liniment to rub on sores.

WHORLED LOOSESTRIFE
Lysimachia quadrifolia
Primrose family (Primulaceae)

Quick ID: Yellow flowers on thin stalks in a whorl around stem; ½" flowers, 5 petals, red ring at base of petals, stamens stick out; 3–6 (but usually 4) 2"–4" leaves whorl around stem at same junction, oval and pointed at both ends; stem smooth to slightly hairy.

Height: 1'–3' **Bloom Season:** June–August

Whorled loosestrife is an easy plant to identify, as both the starlike yellow flowers and the leaves whorl around the stem. The species name, *quadrifolia*, means "four leaves." The curious genus name, *Lysimachia*, honors an ancient king of Sicily named Lysimachus, who purportedly calmed a raging bull with a flower in this family. The common name loosestrife comes from the Greek word *lysis*, which means "to dissolve," and *mache*, which means "strife." Since this plant was thought to have the ability to sooth strife, farmers would place it under the harness of oxen to keep them from fighting. Fringed loosestrife (*L. ciliata*) (inset) has opposite leaves, and the 5 yellow petals are tipped with at least 1 sharp tooth. Look for whorled loosestrife along many Parkway trails, including the Cascades Trail at E. B. Jeffress Park.

BULBOUS BUTTERCUP
Ranunculus bulbosus
Buttercup family (Ranunculaceae)
Quick ID: Glossy yellow flowers on branching, hairy stems; 1" wide, 5 rounded petals, numerous stamens and pistils; basal leaves 1"–4" with long stalks, deeply cut into 3 parts, hairy.

Height: 1'–2' **Bloom Season:** April–June

Introduced from Europe, the base of the stem of bulbous buttercup looks like a bulb. Buttercups are toxic when eaten by cattle and other livestock, but because they have an acidic taste and can cause blisters, they are left uneaten in meadows. For fun, children often hold a buttercup under their chin. A yellow reflection proves that the holder likes butter. The petals of buttercups contain a carotenoid pigment that absorbs blue and green light. The resultant yellow rays are reflected back. The petals have 2 flat surfaces separated by a gap of air that doubles the gloss of the petal, presumably to attract pollinators. About 9 species of buttercup can be found in the park, including kidneyleaf buttercup (*R. abortivus*) and hispid buttercup (*R. hispidus*).

DWARF CINQUEFOIL
Potentilla canadensis
Rose family (Rosaceae)
Quick ID: Small yellow flowers with rounded petals, flower head about ½" wide; alternate leaves have 5 leaflets in the shape of a palm, coarsely toothed; stems silvery-hairy with runners to 18".
Height: 2"–6"   **Bloom Season:** March–May

A low, spreading plant, dwarf cinquefoil resembles a yellow-flowered strawberry plant. The small yellow flowers have 5 rounded petals, and the leaves are divided into 5 leaflets with sharp notches. The name cinquefoil means "five leaves," and they are sometimes called "five fingers" to reflect the hand-like look of the leaves. Dwarf cinquefoils grow on grassy balds and roadsides. Blooming later (April–June), common cinquefoil (*P. simplex*) is very similar to dwarf cinquefoil but the flowers are taller, up to 12", and the leaves are egg-shaped. The much taller rough-fruited cinquefoil (*P. recta*) has light yellow flowers and blooms May–September.

COMMON MULLEIN
Verbascum thapsus
Figwort family (Scrophulariaceae)
Quick ID: Yellow 5-petaled flowers on a very tall thick spike; rosette of large woolly leaves.
Height: 2'–8'   **Bloom Season:** June–September

Wildflower lovers generally don't appreciate introduced species of plants (those that are not native to our country), but early settlers used common mullein in a multitude of ways. Introduced into Virginia in the mid-1700s, common mullein is native to Europe, northern Africa, and Asia. The large woolly leaves work well as warm padding for shoes. The leaves were warmed by the fire and applied to the feet to ease the pain of gout. The soft pliable leaves substituted for toilet paper, and a poultice of leaves was applied to relieve painful hemorrhoids. The seeds of common mullein contain rotenone, which poisons fish and insects and was used as an organic pesticide dust for vegetable crops. Scientists are currently studying the correlation between the use of rotenone and Parkinson's disease.

ROUNDLEAF YELLOW VIOLET
Viola rotundifolia
Violet family (Violaceae)

Quick ID: Bright yellow flowers, 5 petals, 3 lower petals with brownish veins at the base, 2 lateral petals bearded; glossy, rounded notched leaves; flower stalk comes directly from ground.

Height: 2"–5"   **Bloom Season:** March–April

One of the first flowers to bloom in spring, roundleaf yellow violet ushers in the warm weather along with other spring wildflowers, including bloodroot (*Sanguinaria canadensis*), spring beauty (*Claytonia virginica*), and Dutchman's breeches (*Dicentra cucullaria*). Great spangled fritillary butterflies lay their eggs on various violet leaves, including roundleaf yellow violet. Native Americans used yellow violets to make an infusion to drink as a spring tonic and to treat colds, coughs, and dysentery. The leaves and roots were made into a poultice to relieve headaches and to place on boils. They also soaked corn seeds in an infusion of violet roots before planting them to repel insects.

HALBERD-LEAF VIOLET
Viola hastata
Violet family (Violaceae)

Quick ID: Yellow flower, brownish-purple veins on lower petals; flower stem arises from branching stem; long triangular leaves may be variegated silvery-gray between the leaf veins.

Height: 4"–10"   **Bloom Season:** April–May

Halberd-leaf violets have long, triangular, arrow-shaped leaves that are patchy silvery-gray on top. Downy yellow violet (*V. pubescens*) is a stemmed violet with fine hairs on the stem and heart-shaped leaves. Smooth yellow violet (*V. eriocarpa*) resembles downy yellow violet but lacks hairs. The flowers and leaves of violets were used medicinally by early settlers as a cough syrup, a laxative, and as an external poultice for wounds. They were commonly used to make teas, salads, candies, wines, syrups, and jellies. A common folk saying is that when the yellow violets bloom it is time to start hunting for the delicious wild morel mushrooms.

YUCCA
Yucca filamentosa
Agave family (Agavaceae)

Quick ID: Evergreen, stiff, sharply pointed, swordlike leaves 12"–24" and 1"–2" wide, loose threads on leaf margins; creamy white, bell-shaped, 6-petaled, loosely nodding, 2"–2½" flowers hanging from stems; brown upright fruit capsules

Height: 3'–15'   **Bloom Season:** June–September

Yucca, or, as it is commonly called, Adam's needle or Spanish bayonet, is native to the eastern and midwestern states, but it looks as though it would be more at home in the desert than in the mountains of the Blue Ridge Parkway. Native Americans boiled then peeled the leaves into long fibers, which they then braided into cords, baskets, and fishing nets. Containing a soapy compound called saponin, the roots were pounded, boiled, and used as washing soap. The pounded roots were also used as a salve for sores and skin diseases and to intoxicate fish for easy collecting. As it is long-lived, yucca is one of the plants traditionally planted around Appalachian cemeteries to indicate eternal life.

RAMPS
Allium tricoccum
Onion family (Alliaceae)
Quick ID: White flowers in a rounded cluster; 2 or 3 flat, smooth 1" wide leaves 8"–10" with purple at the base.
Height: 6"–20"   **Bloom Season:** June–July

Considered a delicacy in the Appalachians, gathering and eating ramps begins in April and May, culminating in local festivals to celebrate the tasty rite of spring. Locally called "little stinkers," ramps have a strong oniony-garlicky taste and are traditionally cooked in bacon grease and served with potatoes, eggs, ham, beans, and cornbread. Rich in vitamins and minerals, the bulbs of ramps were traditionally eaten as a spring tonic and were believed to thin the blood after the long winter produced harmful "thick" blood. Springtime tonics were thought to help the sluggish blood rise like sap in trees to rejuvenate health. Those who have eaten ramps retain the pungent garlic-onion scent, and schools would occasionally have to close due to the overwhelming aroma in the classroom.

QUEEN ANNE'S LACE
Daucus carota
Umbel family (Apiaceae)
Quick ID: Tiny whitish flowers in slightly curved to flat clusters; deeply dissected leaves; hairy stems.
Height: 1'–3'   **Bloom Season:** May–October

Queen Anne's lace, also called wild carrot, was introduced into North America from Europe. The tiny white flowers are on spindly stalks that all arise from one point, giving the appearance that this group is a single white flower. Botanists call this form an umbel. A single purple flower often occurs in the center of the umbel. Ladies would often press the intricate flower heads between the pages of books to dry like snowflakes in summer. To make a colorful bouquet, children placed the stems of the white flowers in jars of vegetable dye and the next day awoke to a rainbow of color. Queen Anne's lace is similar in appearance to poison hemlock (*Conium maculatum*), which has purple spots on its hairless stem.

COW PARSNIP
Heracleum maximum
Carrot family (Apiaceae)
Quick ID: Large 4"–8" flat clusters of small white flowers; maple-like leaves up to 12"; very tall grooved, hairy stem.
Height: 3'–10'   **Bloom Season:** June–August

Cow parsnip towers above all other flowers on rich, sunny banks lining the Blue Ridge Parkway. Growing up to 10' tall, the flat-topped white flower is found throughout most of the United States except the Gulf Coast and southernmost eastern states. Reaching the size of dinner plates, the flat-topped flower heads resemble gigantic versions of Queen Anne's lace (*Daucus carota*). The large maple-like leaves can reach up to 2' across. Native Americans pounded the roots to make poultices to apply to sores or bruises. The roots were also used to make a yellow dye. Cow parsnip is eaten by white-tailed deer and is favored by cows but is toxic to them.

134

SWEET CICELY
Osmorhiza claytonii
Carrot family (Apiaceae)
Quick ID: Small, white flowers; hairy stem; fernlike leaves, leaflets in 3s and bluntly toothed.
Height: 16"–32"   **Bloom Season:** April–June

The small, inconspicuous white flowers of sweet cicely reach above the fernlike leaves that are bluntly toothed and divided into 3s. Along with the leaves, the roots, which smell like licorice, were added to cooking pots to flavor stews. Native Americans ground the root to use for coughs and sore throats. They also used it for eyewash, as the constant exposure to campfires and smoke often irritated their eyes. Two lookalikes, black snakeroot (*Sanicula* spp.) and honewort (*Cryptotaenia canadensis*), both have leaves less fernlike and don't smell like licorice. The leaves of black snakeroot are palm-shaped and those of honewort are in 3 leaflets. Sweet cicely is found in most areas of the park in rich woods. Near the end of May, look for sweet cicely at the Still House parking area at Milepost 31.4.

WILD SARSAPARILLA
Aralia nudicaulis
Ginseng family (Araliaceae)
Quick ID: Round clusters of 1"–2" greenish-white flowers, flowers under leaves; whorl of 3 leaves in groups of 5 finely serrated leaflets 3"–5" long and 2" wide; leafless stalk.
Height: 8"–20"   **Bloom Season:** May–July

Growing in colonies in rich woods, the flowers of wild sarsaparilla, or false sarsaparilla, are in rounded clusters on upright stems beneath the tall leaves. The greenish-white flowers form 1"–2" round clusters that resemble small golf balls. In late summer the flowers are replaced by dark blue-black berries. The berries were used to make jelly and wine similar in taste to elderberry wine. Wild sarsaparilla is better known as a substitute for the root beer–like drink called sarsaparilla. Mixed with the roots of sassafras (*Sassafras albidum*) and other herbs, root tea and later root beer became popular in the late 1800s. In 1960 the use of sassafras root was banned when scientists discovered that it contained a substance that causes liver damage or cancer. Wild sarsaparilla grows in rich woods in the park.

AMERICAN GINSENG
Panax quinquefolius
Ginseng family (Araliaceae)

Quick ID: Tiny, greenish-white flowers that hide among the leaves; compound leaves with 5 stalked leaflets that are oval and toothed; red berries in fall.

Height: 8"–24"   **Bloom Season:** May–June

No other plant has been as sought after in the wild as American ginseng, or "sang." Residents of the Southern Appalachians traditionally harvested the tuberous roots to sell for supplemental income. The plant was often referred to as "green gold," and the search for ginseng was commonly referred to as "sanging" or "sang digging." Conscientious harvesters would only harvest the older plants and made sure to replant the seeds in the same location. Over-gathering and commercial exploitation of ginseng has caused officials to use methods such as tagging plants to trace poachers of this now-rare plant. Harvesting ginseng from national parklands such as the Blue Ridge Parkway is a federal crime and may result in large fines, even incarceration.

COMMON YARROW
Achillea millefolium
Aster family (Asteraceae)
Quick ID: White or sometimes pink flat-topped clusters of tiny flowers; lacy, fernlike leaves.
Height: 1'–3'
Bloom Season: June–October

One of the most common wildflowers found along the Blue Ridge Parkway, yarrow thrives in disturbed areas much of the year. The lacy, finely
dissected leaves are a good clue to identifying yarrow from some of its
look-alikes, including flowering spurge (*Euphorbia corollata*), Queen
Anne's lace (*Daucus carota*), boneset (*Eupatorium perfoliatum*), and
white snakeroot (*Ageratina altissima*). The mythological Greek warrior
Achilles reportedly used the leaves of yarrow to heal wounds of injured
soldiers. Civil War doctors also used the astringent leaves to stop the
bleeding of wounded soldiers. It has widespread use in folk medicine
to treat inflammation, hemorrhoids, and even baldness. The leaves and
flowers were used to make a yellow dye. A pink version grows in meadows at Mount Mitchell.

WHITE SNAKEROOT
Ageratina altissima
Aster family (Asteraceae)

Quick ID: Flat heads of 12–25 bright white flowers; opposite, oval to heart-shaped leaves with serrated margins on slender stalks.

Height: 1'–4' **Bloom Season:** July–October

Blooming in late summer and fall, the bright white flowers look somewhat like cotton balls on stems. Because this plant contains a toxin called tremetol, deer and other wildlife avoid it. In the 1800s many people, including Abraham Lincoln's mother, were killed by a mysterious malady that no one could identify. The mystery was finally solved by Dr. Anna Pierce Hobbs Bixby, a physician who methodically studied the disease and traced the deaths to consumption of tainted milk and butter from cows or goats eating snakeroot. She had befriended a Shawnee woman, who may have played a key role in the discovery of "milk sickness." Also sporting white flowers but blooming earlier, wild quinine (*Parthenium integrifolium*) was used medicinally to treat fevers, coughs, and sore throats, and its leaves were applied to burns. *A. altissima* var. *roanensis* is an Appalachian endemic snakeroot found only at high elevations.

PLANTAIN-LEAVED PUSSYTOES
Antennaria plantaginifolia
Aster family (Asteraceae)

Quick ID: Clusters of fuzzy white flowers in mats, on top of stem; 1"–3" grayish, paddle-shaped basal leaves with 3 veins, wooly underneath; narrower alternate leaves on the stem.

Height: 4"–16"   **Bloom Season:** March–May

Forming low colonies, pussytoes has white fuzzy-looking flowers that imaginatively resemble cat's paws. Male and female flowers are on different plants. Plantain-leaved pussytoes has basal leaves that look somewhat like the leaves of plantain (*Plantago* spp.). With yellowish-orange tipped stamens, the male flowers are generally on shorter stems than the female flowers. Some colonies may be entirely one sex. Singlehead pussytoes (*A. solitaria*) produces only 1 flower head per stem. Parlin's pussytoes (*A. parlinii*) was first identified by Maine botanist John Crawford Parlin (1863–1948). Look for pussytoes in open areas throughout the park.

140

GREAT INDIAN PLANTAIN
Arnoglossum reniforme
Aster family (Asteraceae)
Quick ID: White flowers in a flat head; grooved stems with purplish tint, 6–8 angles; upper leaves fan-shaped, toothed, green on both sides, kidney-shaped lower leaves.
Height: 3'–9'   **Bloom Season:** June–October

Very tall plants, Indian plantains have large kidney-shaped leaves and broad flat-topped flower heads. Previously known as *Cacalia muhlenbergii*, several name changes have resulted in this plant's current Latin name. Great Indian plantain grows in woodlands and cove forests. The stem of pale Indian plantain (*A. atriplicifolium*) lacks the grooves of great Indian plantain. Pale Indian plantain was used medicinally to make a poultice for wounds and to draw poisonous substances from blood. The dried leaf was powdered and used like salt. Look for great Indian plantain growing along Heintooga Road.

141

COMMON FLEABANE
Erigeron philadelphicus
Aster family (Asteraceae)
Quick ID: White (sometimes pinkish) daisy-like flowers, numerous thin white petals (ray flowers) yellow center (disk flowers); narrow, coarsely toothed, alternate leaves clasp the hairy stem.

Height: 6"–30"   **Bloom Season:** April–August

Fleabanes are white daisy-like plants that grow prolifically on roadsides, meadows, and disturbed places. Like daisies and other members of the Aster family, fleabanes have white ray flowers that surround an inner yellow button of disk flowers. Common or Philadelphia fleabane typically has over 150 white petal-like, very thin ray flowers compared to the 15–35 white ray flowers of oxeye daisy (*Leucanthemum vulgare*). Other fleabanes found here include daisy fleabane (*E. annuus*) and rough fleabane (*E. strigosus*). In the same genus, the lilac-colored flowers of Robin's plantain (*E. pulchellus*) bloom in early spring. Native Americans used fleabane medicinally as an eye medicine and for coughs and colds. It was also boiled and mixed with tallow to be placed on sores, and a poultice was made to help relieve headaches.

BONESET
Eupatorium perfoliatum
Aster family (Asteraceae)
Quick ID: Small white flowers on numerous branching stems; opposite leaves 3"–8", densely hairy beneath, only sparsely hairy above, bases converge around stem; hairy stems.

Height: 2'–5' **Bloom Season:** July–October

Found in wet places and along roadsides, the white flowers of boneset bloom in late summer into fall. Long used as a medicinal plant by Native Americans, a tea was made by boiling the leaves and roots and used to treat sore throats and colds. The tea typically made the sufferer throw up phlegm, helping relieve the symptoms of influenza. Learning from Native Americans of its medicinal use for fevers, early colonists gathered and dried the plant in fall, hanging it in bundles from rafters for future treatment of fevers, especially malaria. Several other white-flowered plants are very similar in appearance to boneset, but a close look at the leaves often can help separate them. Upland boneset (*E. sessilifolium*) has narrow, stalkless leaves; hyssopleaf thoroughwort (*E. hyssopifolium*) has linear leaves in whorls of 4.

BLUE RIDGE WHITE HEART-LEAVED ASTER
Eurybia chlorolepis
Aster family (Asteraceae)

Quick ID: White-petaled flowers with yellow center; alternate, heart-shaped leaves sharply serrated; stem becomes woody with age.

Height: 10"–31"   **Bloom Season:** August–October

Blue Ridge white heart-leaved aster is a Southern Appalachian endemic found along the Blue Ridge Parkway in southwestern Virginia through western North Carolina. It occurs in spruce-fir forests at high altitudes about 4,000'–6,500'. The similar and widespread white wood aster (*E. divaricata*) has fewer white petals and occurs at lower elevations, below 4,000'. In 1994 DNA evidence showed clearly that there were large genetic distinctions in European and Asian asters and the North American asters. Taxonomists then divided the genus Aster into several separate genera, including *Eurybia*, *Symphyotrichum*, and *Doellingeria*. Appalachian flat-topped white aster (*Doellingeria infirma*) (inset) has 5–14 white ray flowers and slender single stems that branch at the top.

144

OXEYE DAISY
Leucanthemum vulgare
Aster family (Asteraceae)
Quick ID: White flowers with yellow center; narrow, irregularly toothed, lobed 2"–6" leaves, linear and reduced in size up the stem.
Height: 12"–30" **Bloom Season:** April–October

The blossom with romantic overtures, the petals of oxeye daisy are well known as the loves-me-loves-me-not flower. Introduced to North America from Europe, the lovely white flowers can now be found growing along roadsides, in pastures, and in disturbed areas. Like other members of the Aster family, the flower head is composed of central yellow disk flowers surrounded by narrow white ray flowers that resemble individual petals. The Latin name has been recently changed from *Chrysanthemum leucanthemum*. Oxeye daisy is one of the flowers that you can find blooming throughout the seasons along the Parkway.

RABBIT TOBACCO
Pseudognaphalium obtusifolium
Aster family (Asteraceae)

Quick ID: White to pale yellowish flowers that look unopened at top of stem; alternate, woolly 1"–3" leaves, narrow and pointed; cottony stem.

Height: 12"–36"   **Bloom Season:** August–November

Rabbit tobacco, or sweet everlasting, is an unusual-looking flower that always looks as though it has unopened white buds at the top of the stem. When you touch the flowers, they feel dry due to the tiny flowers being covered on the outside by layers of pointed white bracts. The flowers are often used to make dried flower arrangements, hence the name "everlasting." These fragrant flowers smell like peppery maple syrup or sweet tobacco when rubbed. Native Americans used the plant for many medicinal uses. The dried leaves were smoked in a pipe to calm asthmatic episodes. It was also used in a sweat bath for various diseases. The leaves were chewed for a sore throat or mouth and soaked in water or other liquid for use as a cough syrup. The plant was recently moved from the genus *Gnaphalium* to *Pseudognaphalium*.

UMBRELLA LEAF
Diphylleia cymosa
Barberry family (Berberidaceae)

Quick ID: Small, rounded, 6-petaled white flowers in cluster at end of stem; 2 maple-like leaves 12"–24" across with pointed, coarsely toothed lobes; dark blue berries on bright red stalks.

Height: 1'–3'   **Bloom Season:** April–June

Small clusters of white flowers standing tall above 2 large maple-like leaves identify this plant as umbrella leaf. In the same family as mayapple (*Podophyllum peltatum*), umbrella leaf is the only representative of the genus *Diphylleia* in North America. The other 2 species are found in Japan and China. Visitors to the Blue Ridge Parkway have an opportunity to see this significant Southern Appalachian endemic. May is a good time to look

for the white blooms, especially in seepage areas and along small streams such as those along the Tanawha Trail near Linn Cove Viaduct Visitor Center. In fall it is easy to identify this plant from the deep blue berries that are held atop bright red stalks.

MAYAPPLE
Podophyllum peltatum
Barberry family (Berberidaceae)
Quick ID: A single nodding 2" flower with 6–9 waxy white petals in the axil between the 2 leaves; 2 umbrella-like 8"–15" leaves with 5–9 deep lobes; yellow 1"–1½" egg-shaped fruits.
Height: 12"–18"   **Bloom Season:** April–May

Growing in moist areas such as along the James River, at Mabry Mill, and along the Rattlesnake Lodge Trail, where large colonies form, the white flower of mayapple, or American mandrake, hides beneath 2 dinner plate–size leaves. A loner here, the only other flower in this genus is found in East Asia. In August yellow apple-like fruits are edible, but all other parts of the plant are toxic. Plants have developed toxins to avoid predation, but sometimes these toxins can be used for medicinal purposes. The Cherokee used the root as a laxative and to rid the body of worms. It has also been used to treat warts and cancers. A chemical found in the root has cytotoxic anticancer properties and is currently being used in treating testicular and lung cancers.

CUTLEAF TOOTHWORT
Cardamine concatenata
Mustard family (Brassicaceae)
Quick ID: White to pinkish bell-shaped flowers with 4 oval petals; coarsely toothed leaves in whorls of 3.
Height: 8"–16"   **Bloom Season:** March–May

Along the Blue Ridge Parkway, early bloomers called spring ephemerals flower quickly and fade away in the short window of time before tree leaves shadow the understory. One of these ephemerals is cutleaf toothwort, whose delicate white to pinkish flowers balance atop a whorl of deeply cut leaves. The root, called a rhizome, has toothlike projections that prompted early physicians to use the powdered root to cure toothaches. The leaves were eaten as a spring herb, and the root was used like pepper. Another similar toothwort, crinkleroot or broadleaf toothwort (*C. diphylla*) (inset), can more commonly be found in the southern sections of the Parkway, such as along the Linville Falls Trail. In some books and field guides, you may find cutleaf toothwort listed under its previous Latin name, *Dentaria lanciniata*.

STARRY CAMPION
Silene stellata
Pink family (Caryophyllaceae)

Quick ID: White, star-shaped flowers, 5 fringed petals united at the base, woolly at the inflated base, bell-shaped; oval leaves in whorls of 4; thin, weak stem.

Height: 12"–48"   **Bloom Season:** July–September

Both the native starry campion and its introduced cousin from Europe, bladder campion (*S. vulgaris*) can be found along the Blue Ridge Parkway. The thin, weak stem of starry campion often looks like a vine, and the plant may droop over fences or other plants. Look for starry campion along Heintooga Spur Road. Bladder campion lacks the feathery fringes of the native starry campion but boasts an inflated pink-striped pouch just below the 5 deeply notched petals. Bladder campion was probably introduced from Europe as a food source, as the leaves are commonly cooked and eaten in the Mediterranean region. Bladder campion can be found along roadsides or along trails, such as near Mabry Mill.

STAR CHICKWEED
Stellaria pubera
Pink family (Caryophyllaceae)
Quick ID: White starlike flowers, 5 deeply notched petals; hairy stems; opposite, elliptical leaves.
Height: 6"–16"   **Bloom Season:** March–May

Star chickweed is such a common small wildflower that it is often passed by without a glance. But upon closer inspection, the small flowers are quite lovely. Giving the appearance of having 10 petals, the actual 5 petals are so deeply notched that they fool even the most observant. Herbalists used the leaves to make a poultice to relieve swellings, hemorrhoids, and for skin sores. The small seeds are eaten by birds. The young leaves can be cooked and eaten like greens. The endemic Tennessee chickweed (*S. corei*) (inset) has much longer sepals than those of star chickweed.

151

MOUNTAIN STONECROP
Sedum ternatum
Stonecrop family (Crassulaceae)

Quick ID: White, starry flowers on curved horizontal branches, 5 sharply pointed petals; thick, fleshy, spatula-shaped leaves whorled in 3s or 4s; low-lying stems that send up erect stalks.

Height: 4"–8"   **Bloom Season:** April–June

Most gardeners are familiar with sedums; many colorful varieties of these plants are commonly chosen as a home rock garden groundcover. In the wild, mountain stonecrop is our most common native sedum. Growing on rocky outcrops and cliffs where few other plants can survive, sedums are well adapted to withstand the harsh conditions these habitats deliver. In spring the starry white flowers are borne on curved branches that arch over the fleshy, water-retaining leaves. Sharing similar habitats, cliff stonecrop (*S. glaucophyllum*), which has alternate leaves, is an Appalachian endemic, as is the pink-flowered Allegheny live-forever (*Hylotelephium telephioides*). Please be careful where you put your feet when hiking on rocky areas where this and other sensitive plants may be damaged.

APPALACHIAN BEAKED DODDER
Cuscuta rostrata
Morning-glory family (Convolvulaceae)
Quick ID: Tiny whitish to yellowish-orange, bell-shaped flowers; vine encircling other plants; scale-like leaves.

Height: Varies   **Bloom Season:** July–September

Dodders are parasitic plants that are often described as looking like someone threw long strands of thin orange spaghetti all over another plant. Many colorful common names have been given to describe these vines, including love vine, witch's shoestrings, witch's hair, strangle weed, and devil's hair. These unusual plants start life with shallow roots, but these soon die away and the plant becomes entirely dependent on other plants for its nourishment because it does not produce its own chlorophyll. These parasitic vines stealthily send out tendrils that cling to another plant and encircle it counterclockwise. The vine then presses little bumps called haustoria into the host plant, which allow it to leach out the nutrients it needs to survive.

GALAX
Galax urceolata
Diapensia family (Diapensiaceae)
Quick ID: Up to 20" single spike of small white flowers; long, thin stalk; dark green rounded to heart-shaped, shiny, 2"–5" toothed leaves.
Height: 18"–24"   **Bloom Season:** May–July

Often found growing with mountain laurel or great rhododendron shrubs, galax is recognized by the tall spikes adorned with small white flowers that rise above shiny green leaves. Thriving in the cool, moist Appalachian forests, galax spreads luxuriously by underground roots called rhizomes. With the arrival of fall and cooler temperatures, the tough, leathery leaves turn bronzy reddish-purple, carpeting the understory with rich color. Galax is native to the Appalachian Mountains, and its leaves have long been prized for use in floral arrangements. Many mountain people traditionally relied on the sale of galax leaves as a source of income. Along with American ginseng (*Panax quinquefolia*), galax poaching has risen at an alarming rate, threatening their populations. Make sure to alert a park official if you suspect illegal harvesting of these or any other plants.

ROUNDLEAF SUNDEW
Drosera rotundifolia
Sundew family (Droseraceae)

Quick ID: Small white 5-petaled flowers that grow on one side of a leafless stalk; basal rosette of round leaves with reddish, sticky, glistening hairs on the leaf edge.

Height: 4"–9"   **Bloom Season:** July–September

Growing in bogs and vertical seepage areas in the mountains of the Blue Ridge Parkway, roundleaf sundew is an unusual plant. Sundews are carnivorous plants, deriving some of their nutrients from insects, which they catch in sticky glandular secretions. The leaves of sundews were used to make cheese in Sweden. The leaves have also been used by Native Americans to treat warts. Sundew has been widely used to treat coughs, including whooping cough. Sundews are widely used in folk medicines around the world, and studies have shown them to have antibacterial and anti-inflammatory properties. Found across the Northern Hemisphere, roundleaf sundew is threatened or endangered in some areas due to habitat loss and over-collection.

STRIPED WINTERGREEN
Chimaphila maculata
Heath family (Ericaceae)

Quick ID: Evergreen; white, waxy nodding flowers at the top of a thin reddish stem, 5 rounded petals, round green center; alternate, lance-shaped 1½"–2" leaves with white or greenish stripes along the major veins; dark brown woody fruits on stem split into 5 sections.

Height: 4"–10" **Bloom Season:** May–June

In summer the sweet-smelling waxy-looking white flowers of striped, or spotted, wintergreen nod from a spindly stem. Found in dry woods along the Parkway, the evergreen leaves have conspicuous white stripes all year and in winter turn purplish green. The genus name, *Chimaphila*, means "winter lover," as the dark green leaves and brown fruit capsule remain throughout the cold winter months. Settlers to the area sometimes called this plant rheumatism root and used it to treat aching joints. Native Americans used it as a wash for cancers, ulcers, and ringworm. They called the plant pipsissewa, which means "to break into pieces," as they used the plant to treat kidney stones.

WINTERGREEN
Gaultheria procumbens
Heath family (Ericaceae)
Quick ID: Evergreen; white bell-shaped, nodding flowers; thick, oval leaves with shallow teeth; bright red berries.
Height: 2"–6"   **Bloom Season:** July–August

Blooming in summer, the small white bell-shaped flowers delicately hang beneath the leaves of wintergreen, or teaberry. Sometimes described as being "sealing-wax red," the dry berries that replace the flowers are often more noticeable than the flowers, especially as they often last into winter. Often called teaberry, the minty leaves were used to flavor tea, chewing gum, candy, and medicines. The dried leaves were also used as a chewing tobacco substitute. The leaves contain methyl salicylate, which is closely related to aspirin. An essential oil made from the leaves was used to treat the aches and pains of arthritis. Chipmunks and squirrels enjoy the tasty berries in winter, and deer browse on the leaves. The genus name, *Gaultheria*, honors Canadian botanist Dr. Jean-François Gaulthier (1708–1756).

INDIAN PIPE
Monotropa uniflora
Heath family (Ericaceae)
Quick ID: Translucent waxy white flower and stem; nodding urn-shaped flowers; blackens with age.
Height: 2"–10"   **Bloom Season:** June–September

Few plants arouse curiosity and fear at the same time, but Indian pipe often does. Rising silently from the damp, dark forest floor, the white urn-shaped flower nods atop a translucent, waxy stem. It is no wonder this flower has been dubbed ghost flower, ice plant, and corpse plant—it has an uncanny resemblance to an underworldly smoking pipe thrust from the grave. Regardless of its appearance, Cherokees used this flower medicinally as an effective wash to relieve sore eyes. The ground-up roots were given to children to calm epileptic seizures and convulsions. In 1836 John Gunn mentioned in his book *The New Domestic Physician or Home Book of Health* that Indian pipe was used as a substitute for opium, as it relieved restlessness and irritability.

158

GREAT RHODODENDRON
Rhododendron maximum
Heath family (Ericaceae)

Quick ID: Large evergreen shrub; white flowers with pinkish tinge and usually some green dots; 3"–14" large leathery oblong leaves with rolled edges, whitish underneath.

Height: 10'–30' **Bloom Season:** June–August

Known locally as laurel, great laurel, or rosebay rhododendron, great rhododendron is one of the most common rhododendrons in the Southern Appalachians, with thickets of dense plants following streams and filling rich coves with their characteristic pink-tinged white blooms. Visitors to the Blue Ridge Parkway who miss the earlier pink blooms of the Catawba rhododendrons can enjoy driving and hiking through inspiring great rhododendron thickets. Although bloom times vary from year to year, depending on elevation, most plants start blooming in late June into July. The Mabry Mill area is a good place to see these lovely evergreen shrubs at their best.

FLOWERING SPURGE
Euphorbia corollata
Euphorbia family (Euphorbiaceae)
Quick ID: Small white, flat flowers, 5 petals (bracts); 1½" linear to oblong thick leaves, whorled or alternate.
Height: 20"–40"   **Bloom Season:** June–September

One of the most famous members of the Euphorbia family grows wild in many parts of the world, but here we know it as the Christmas poinsettia. Native to the eastern and central states, flowering spurge is a unique plant that grows wild in open fields, dry woods, and roadsides. Members of this family have milky latex in the stems that is irritating to the skin and may cause blistering if handled. Native Americans commonly used the milky juice to remove warts, sores, pimples, and other skin growths. They ground the roots to place on a rotten tooth to relieve the toothache. True to its common name, spurge, it was used to purge a hapless patient.

SQUIRREL CORN
Dicentra canadensis
Fumitory family (Fumariaceae)
Quick ID: Pinkish-white heart-shaped flowers; vertical stalk; finely dissected leaves, often with a whitish bloom.
Height: 4"–12"   **Bloom Season:** April–May

Often confused with the similar Dutchman's breeches (*D. cucullaria*), squirrel corn does not have the tiny inverted leggings. Instead this fragrant early-spring bloomer is heart-shaped. A more appropriate name for this flower might be "white valentine," as the flowers resemble miniature puffy hearts. The name squirrel corn comes from the small underground bulblets, or corms, that look like kernels of corn and are eaten by squirrels, chipmunks, mice, and wild turkeys. The corms contain a chemical called corydalis that was used to treat skin disease and syphilis. Look for squirrel corn along trails in rich woods.

DUTCHMAN'S BREECHES

Dicentra cucullaria
Fumitory family (Fumariaceae)
Quick ID: Waxy, white, yellow-tipped flowers that resemble tiny pantaloons; arching stem; leaves highly dissected, resembling parsley.
Height: 5"–9"   **Bloom Season:** April–May

Like a clothesline full of puffy pantaloons, the billowy white blooms of Dutchman's breeches resemble tiny upside-down pants that have 2 plump legs tipped with a lacy yellow waistband. Dutchman's breeches is related to squirrel corn (*D. canadensis*) and wild bleeding heart (*D. eximia*). These three plants have been reassigned from the Poppy family to the Fumitory family, as all members of this family have symmetrical flowers, while those in the Poppy family do not. If you look closely at the white flowers, you may notice that they are often punched with tiny holes. Large bumblebees can reach the nectar reward hidden deep within the flowers, but smaller bees must punch a hole in the base of the flower to reach the nectar.

FRINGED PHACELIA
Phacelia fimbriata
Waterleaf family (Hydrophyllaceae)
Quick ID: 5–15 flowers; 5 white to pale lavender, fringed petals, lavender anthers; weak stems with hairs that stand straight out; 2" whitish leaves with broad lobes, upper leaves unstalked, lower leaves stalked.
Height: 8"–16"   **Bloom Season:** April–June

From a distance, large colonies of fringed phacelia, or Blue Ridge phacelia, cover the ground like blankets of sparkling snow. Endemic to the Southern Appalachians, fringed phacelia is abundant in nearby Great Smoky Mountains but has a limited distribution elsewhere. Along the Parkway it can be found near Grandfather Mountain. The very similar Miami mist (*P. purshii*) has pale lavender fringed flowers with white centers and hairs that press closely against the stem. The stems of Miami mist also tend to be upright rather than the thin, prostrate stems that barely hold fringed phacelia. Also sporting lavender flowers, fernleaf phacelia (*P. bipinnatifida*), lacks fringes, and Virginia waterleaf (*Hydrophyllum virginianum*) has bell-shaped flowers with long stamens.

163

DEVIL'S BIT
Chamaelirium luteum
Bunchflower family (Melanthiaceae)
Quick ID: Thin, dense 5" spike of tiny white flowers; wand-like stem; smooth elongated leaves.
Height: 1'–3'   **Bloom Season:** May–July

Also known as fairy wand or false unicorn, the long gracefully arching flowers of the devil's bit resemble a wand or, with imagination, the horn of a unicorn. Growing in rich forests, the plants of devil's bit are either male or female. The male flowers are white with yellow stamens; when mature, they take on a creamy coloration and tend to droop at the tip. The female flowers are greenish-white in dense terminal spikes. Although devil's bit it is not a lily and does not lie on the ground, the genus name, *Chamaelirium*, means "ground lily." The species name, *luteum*, means "yellow," referring to the yellowish color of the male flowers. Look for devil's bit along the trail to Linville Falls.

SPECKLED WOOD LILY
Clintonia umbellulata
Lily family (Liliaceae)

Quick ID: White cluster of tiny flowers at the end of a single stalk, flowers often with purplish spots; leafless, hairy stalk; 3–4 flat leaves, 6"–12" long with central "fold," 1"–3½" wide with hairy fringes at the base; stemmed round, blackish fruits in a ball.

Height: 8"–15"   **Bloom Season:** May–June

The small white flowers of speckled wood lily are also known as white Clintonia and blackbead lily. Sitting atop a thin, downy stalk, the rounded clusters of white flowers are often speckled with green and purple spots. Speckled wood lily's closest relative along the Parkway, bluebead lily (*C. borealis*), is found in high-altitude areas. Bluebead lily has greenish-yellow, bell-shaped flowers and bright blue berries, while speckled wood lily has white flowers and very dark blue-black berries. Without the flowers or fruits, you can look for the hairs on the leaf margins of speckled wood lily, which are lacking on the leaves of bluebead lily. At the end of May or the first part of June, look for this Appalachian endemic along the Mountains-to-Sea Trail in the southern part of the Parkway.

FALSE SOLOMON'S SEAL

Maianthemum racemosum
Ruscus family (Ruscaceae)

Quick ID: Arching, unbranched, slightly zigzagged stem; alternate, elliptic, 3"–6" leaves with obvious parallel veins in 2 rows along the stem; tiny white starlike flowers on multiple stems at tip of main stem; fruits are round green berries with red splotches, turning reddish.

Height: 16"–32"

Bloom Season: April–July

In the dappled shade of woodland areas along the Parkway, the bright white flowers of false Solomon's seal joust with passing breezes. This plant is sometimes confused with Solomon's seal (*Polygonatum biflorum*), as the arching stems are conspicuous on both these plants. If they are in flower or fruit, the identification is easy—the white flowers of false Solomon's seal are gathered in a pyramid shaped cluster at the tip of the stem, while the greenish-white bell-shaped flowers of Solomon's seal hang delicately below the leaves of the arching stem. Bees and other insects visit the sweet-smelling flowers. In fall the reddish fruits attract wildlife such as birds, chipmunks, and squirrels.

FLY POISON
Amianthium muscaetoxicum
Bunchflower family (Melanthiaceae)
Quick ID: White star-shaped cluster of flowers on tall stem turn greenish after pollination; strap-like leaves up to 16".
Height: 1'–3'   **Bloom Season:** June–July

A wild beauty in open wooded areas, fly poison graces many hiking trails along the Parkway. The white flowers bloom from the bottom upward, and after they are pollinated by butterflies or other insects, the flowers turn green. A few hundred years ago, it was a common practice to dig the bulbs of this plant not for food but to kill flies in the home. The bulb was crushed and mixed with molasses to attract flies to a fatal meal. So effective is the toxin that the common name of this beautiful member of the lily order became fly poison. It was also used by Native Americans to poison crows that damaged their crops. The species name, *muscaetoxicum*, is from the Latin word *muscae* ("flies") and *toxicum* ("poison").

FEATHERBELLS
Stenanthium gramineum
Bunchflower family (Melanthiaceae)
Quick ID: White starlike flowers in 1'–2' cluster on stem, 6 narrow pointed petals (3 petals, 3 sepals); grasslike leaves with depressed line in middle and most numerous near the base; lower stems often curve downward.
Height: 12"–60"   **Bloom Season:** May–August

On graceful stems, the wispy flowers of featherbells can reach up to nearly 5' tall. The drooping stems and starry white flowers give the plant the appearance of a fountain of Fourth-of-July fireworks. The narrow, pointed petals give the flowers a feathery appearance. The genus name, *Stenanthium*, means "narrow flower"; the species name, *gramineum*, means "grasslike," referring to the leaves. Featherbells prefers moist meadows and roadsides such as along Heintooga Road in the southern section of the Parkway. It is sometimes confused with devil's bit (*Chamaelirium luteum*), but the flowers of devil's bit are densely packed around the stem.

PINE BARRENS DEATHCAMAS
Stenanthium leimanthoides
Bunchflower family (Melanthiaceae)
Quick ID: Many creamy-white starlike flowers on solitary tall stem, 6 petals (3 petals, 3 sepals), yellow center; linear leaves 8"–20" at base (but not forming a clump), alternate stem leaves get smaller as they go up the stem.
Height: 2'–5'   **Bloom Season:** June–August

In the same family as fly poison (*Amianthium muscaetoxicum*), pine barrens deathcamas grows on high-elevation rock outcrops and balds. Recently changed from the genus *Zigadenus* to *Stenanthium*, pine barrens deathcamas has an interesting association with sand myrtle (*Kalmia buxifolia*) and turkey beard (*Xerophyllum asphodeloides*). All 3 of these relatively unusual plants are found near sea level in the pine barrens of New Jersey and at over 6,000' elevation on the summit of Grandfather Mountain. All parts of the plant are toxic, containing alkaloids that produce slow heart and breathing rates; ingestion is potentially lethal.

DOWNY RATTLESNAKE ORCHID
Goodyera pubescens
Orchid family (Orchidaceae)

Quick ID: Small white flowers with saclike lower lip on single spike; 4–8 evergreen basal leaves with strong white central midline and white veins that form loose "checkers."

Height: 6"–16"   **Bloom Season:** June–August

Downy rattlesnake orchid is historically called downy rattlesnake plantain. The small white flowers are borne around the top of a relatively thick stalk. The unique snakeskin pattern etched on the dark green leaves led to its use to treat snakebites. After flowering, many tiny seeds are produced, but their survival depends on finding a particular soil fungus for germination and nutrients. The similar but less common lesser rattlesnake orchid (*G. repens*) is also found in the park, hiding quietly under hemlocks and other conifers. This orchid is smaller and typically has flowers that are more loosely oriented to one side. The leaves of this more northern species lack a central white midline and are reticulate rather than checkered. Look for both species on the Flat Rock Trail, Milepost 308.2.

YELLOW NODDING LADIES' TRESSES
Spiranthes ochroleuca
Orchid family (Orchidaceae)
Quick ID: Spike of small off-white flowers, underside of the lower lip butterscotch colored; small, narrow, alternate leaves that clasp stalk.
Height: 8"–20"   **Bloom Season:** September–October

In September and October, the Parkway comes alive with color as the forests prepare for winter in a spectacular finale. Often overlooked in this fall splendor are the thin stalks of yellow nodding ladies' tresses. These miniature marvels of beauty are tiny, perfectly formed orchids that spiral up a thin stalk. The tiny white flowers that twinkle in the sunlight can be seen at higher elevations along the Parkway, including areas near Mount Pisgah, Julian Price Park, Linville Falls, and Richland Balsam. It occurs in relatively dry open sites, often with stiff gentian (*Gentianella quinquefolia*), various club mosses, and the uncommon fern ally *Botrychium multifidum*. Several other species are found here, including southern slender ladies' tresses (*S. lacera*) in dry areas and nodding ladies' tresses (*S. cernua*) in wetlands.

171

BLOODROOT
Sanguinaria canadensis
Poppy family (Papaveraceae)
Quick ID: Single flower, 1"–2" across, with 8–12 white petals, yellow stamens; single leaf, deeply lobed.
Height: 2"–6"   **Bloom Season:** March–May

Bloodroot is well known to wildflower enthusiasts as a champion of spring wildflowers, as its crisp white daisy-like petals unfailingly decorate forests and trails in March and April. Used as a dye by American Indians the stem and roots of this beauty contain juice the color of blood, hence the name bloodroot. The root was also used to treat ulcers, skin sores, and skin cancers. Once used as an antibacterial in toothpaste, current research suggests that the plant actually causes precancerous lesions. The sap contains a strong alkaloid called sanguinarine that destroys cells and is currently being studied for its possible use in cancer treatments. The delicate white flowers remain only a few days, but the single wavy-lobed leaf remains throughout spring.

POKEWEED
Phytolacca americana
Pokeweed family (Phytolaccaceae)
Quick ID: Large, shrub-like plant; reddish stems; large 5"–12" oval leaves; white flowers on spikes; berries green, turning to shiny dark purple.
Height: 4'–10'   **Bloom Season:** July–October

Considered a weed, pokeweed, or simply "poke," is a well-known plant of waysides, fencerows, and waste places. Local people harvest the tender young shoots and leaves for food. Even though all parts of the plant are toxic, the secret to eating poke "sallet" safely is to cook the tender young stems like asparagus, drain and rinse, cook them again, and for good measure repeat the steps a third time. The dark purple berries were gathered in late summer to make ink and to dye cloth. A poke root wash was used to combat the itch from the mite that causes scabies. To ease the pain of rheumatism, sufferers relied on pokeberry tinctures or drank pokeberry tea or wine.

WHITE TURTLEHEAD
Chelone glabra
Plantain family (Plantaginaceae)
Quick ID: White flowers with 2 lips sometimes tinged with pink; opposite, lance-shaped, serrated leaves, 4"–6" with short stalk.

Height: 20"–36"　　　　　　　　　　　　**Bloom Season:** July–September

Found in wet areas, white turtlehead is known by an abundance of common names, including balmony, snakehead, and fish mouth, which all describe the unique shape of the flower. Along with large bees that pollinate the flowers, territorial ruby-throated hummingbirds will vigorously defend these plants from intruders. Turtlehead is also the only food source for the Baltimore checkerspot butterfly larvae. Early settlers used the bitter leaves medicinally as a tonic and a laxative. Sometimes mixed with yellow root (*Xanthorhiza simplicissima*) and tulip poplar bark, a tablespoonful of the dried flowers were steeped in hot water and sipped to remove the yellow skin and eye coloration caused by jaundice. It was also given to children to rid them of worms.

DOLL'S EYES
Actaea pachypoda
Buttercup family (Ranunculaceae)
Quick ID: Small, white, starry flowers at end of stem; leaves divided into leaflets; round white fruits with single dark dot at tip at end of red stalk.
Height: 16"–32"   **Bloom Season:** April–June

In spring the delicate starry flowers of doll's eyes, or white baneberry, go unnoticed as hikers pass them by on trails along the Parkway. However, in September and October this plant commands attention; upon close inspection the pea-size white berries have 1 dark dot at the end that looks uncannily like an eye. The berries resemble the porcelain eyes that were placed in china dolls in the 1800s, prompting the common name of doll's eyes for this plant. The common name white baneberry comes from the toxicity of the berries, which can cause severe diarrhea, dizziness, and hallucinations. Look for doll's eyes throughout the Parkway and in the Doughton Park campground.

WOOD ANEMONE
Anemone quinquefolia
Buttercup family (Ranunculaceae)
Quick ID: 5 delicate, bright white petal-like sepals; whorl of 3 stalked leaves; deeply cut leaves appear to be divided into 3–5 leaflets.
Height: 4"–8"   **Bloom Season:** April–June

In early spring, wood anemone is frequently found along woodland Parkway trails. *Anemone* comes from the Anemoi, Greek wind gods, which suits this flower well, as they bloom with the warm spring winds. Along with wood anemones, other members of the Buttercup family have showy sepals and lack true petals. Another plant in this genus, thimbleweed (*Anemone virginiana*), is much taller and blooms later in summer. Reaching up to 3', thimbleweed has long stalks supporting a single white flower with a yellow button-like center. The leaves are divided into 3 segments, somewhat like maple leaves.

BLACK COHOSH

Actaea racemosa

Buttercup family (Ranunculaceae)

Quick ID: ½" white flower with numerous "fuzzy" white stamens; flowers on spikes about 12" long; tall pliable stems; coarsely toothed leaves with 3 leaflets.

Height: 3'–8'   **Bloom Season:** June–September

Found in shaded clearings in rich Appalachian forests, the tall white-flowered spikes of black cohosh wave gracefully in warm summer breezes. Long used medicinally to treat fevers, bronchitis, and rheumatism, black cohosh was a main ingredient of the "snake-oil" touted by traveling sales-men as a cure-all. It was also used to treat snakebites, earning it the com-mon names of black snakeroot and rattlesnake root. It is currently used as an herbal supplement for menopausal symptoms, but the safety and efficacy of this plant have not been confirmed. Black cohosh is the only known host plant for the Appalachian azure butterfly. If you are obser-vant, you may see these small pale blue butterflies laying their eggs on the flower buds, which provide a ready-made meal for the caterpillars when they hatch.

VIRGIN'S BOWER
Clematis virginiana
Buttercup family (Ranunculaceae)
Quick ID: Vine; 4-petaled starlike white flowers, white anthers; opposite leaves with 3 sharply toothed leaflets.
Height: 2'–10'   **Bloom Season:** July–September

One of the most common roadside flowers in late summer, virgin's bower trails its long vine over fencerows and shrubs, filling with the air with its sweet fragrance. The vines are jam-packed with starry white flowers that attract pollinators such as bees. In fall the white flowers are followed by grayish plumes of feathery seeds that resemble large powder puffs, spawning the common names old man's beard and devil's darning needles. All parts of the plant are poisonous, and severe skin irritation can occur after touching the plant.

In spite of this, Native Americans used an infusion of virgin's bower and milkweed for backaches. It was also used as a medicinal ingredient during the Green Corn Ceremony, when the annual corn harvest was celebrated.

TALL MEADOWRUE
Thalictrum pubescens
Buttercup family (Ranunculaceae)

Quick ID: Plume-like clusters of small whitish to greenish-purple flowers, flowers lacking petals; male and female flowers on same plant, male flowers have numerous erect white stamens; alternate leaves, divided into rounded, 3-lobed leaflets.

Height: 2'–8'   **Bloom Season:** May–July

Meadowrues are placed in the genus *Thalictrum*, in reference to the similarity of their leaves to those of an unrelated European plant, *Ruta graveolens*, commonly called rue. Long used for their medicinal properties in China, these plants may show promise in the development of new pharmaceuticals. Over 20 of the 120 worldwide species are native to North America. Tall meadowrue, or king-of-the-meadow, is found in most of the eastern states into Canada. Blooming April–May, early meadowrue (*T. dioicum*) is about 8"–30" tall and has the male and female flowers on separate plants. The male flowers have gracefully drooping, pale yellow stamens; the female flowers have greenish to purplish pistils. An Appalachian endemic, Mountain meadowrue (*T. clavatum*) (inset) grows up to 2' tall and flowers from spring into summer.

179

RUE ANEMONE
Thalictrum thalictroides
Buttercup family (Ranunculaceae)
Quick ID: Delicate white flowers, 5–10 petal-like sepals; round-lobed 3-parted leaflets; thin, flexible stem.

Height: 4"–8"   **Bloom Season:** March–May

Rue anemone, or windflower, is one of many early-blooming wildflowers called spring ephemerals that bloom before the trees get their leaves. Often found growing in the same habitat as wood anemone (*Anemone quinquefolia*), the white flowers of rue anemone are very similar in appearance. Both plants have flowers with white sepals that look like petals, but rue anemone has 2–3 flowers as opposed to the single flower of wood anemone. The rounded leaves of rue anemone also help to separate it from wood anemone, which has pointed leaves. They may also be confused with bloodroot (*Sanguinaria canadensis*) or round lobed hepatica (*Anemone americana*), both of which have distinctive leaves.

CAROLINA BUGBANE
Trautvetteria caroliniensis
Buttercup family (Ranunculaceae)

Quick ID: White flowers about ½" wide, petals absent, numerous white stamens, green center; stemmed basal leaves deeply divided into 3–11 lobes, irregularly toothed, to 12" wide, alternate stem leaves smaller, with reduced to no stems.

Height: 2'–4'   **Bloom Season:** June–July

Carolina bugbane is also commonly known as tassel rue and false bug-bane. The unusual flowers of Carolina bugbane lack petals, but the numerous bright white stamens serve to attract pollinators. The genus, *Trautvetteria*, is named to honor German botanist Ernst Rudolf von Trautvetter (1908–1889). The common name bugbane is in reference to a western plant called bugbane (*Actaea elata*), which it somewhat resembles. Like most members of the Buttercup family, this plant contains a toxin called protoanemonin, which causes blistering. Some Native Americans applied the strong sap of this plant to "heal" boils. In late June or early July, you can see Carolina bugbane blooming in the wet areas along the trail at Mabry Mill.

GOAT'S BEARD
Aruncus dioicus
Rose family (Rosaceae)
Quick ID: Arching plumes of tiny, creamy-white 5-petaled flowers; alternate, compound leaves with double-toothed edges.
Height: 3'–6'   **Bloom Season:** May–July

In early summer, impressive roadside displays of the feathery white plumes of goat's beard line Parkway roadsides. Also called bride's feathers, the male and female flowers are borne on separate plants. Producing numerous stamens per flower, the males produce a showier bloom than the less-extravagant female plants, with only 3 parts per flower. Often growing in dense colonies, goat's beard can be seen under dappled shade in rich, moist, wooded areas. In June look for goat's beard blooming at Milepost 279. Native Americans beat the root to apply to bee stings, and an infusion was used to bathe swollen feet. Goat's beard is sometimes confused with false goat's beard, but Appalachian false goat's beard (*Astilbe biternata*) has hairy stems, and the end leaflets are lobed.

WILD STRAWBERRY
Fragaria virginiana
Rose family (Rosaceae)
Quick ID: White flowers, 5 rounded petals, yellow stamens; 3 toothed leaflets; creeping stems; red fruits.
Height: 1"–4"　　　　　　　　　　　　**Bloom Season:** April–June

Native to eastern North America, wild strawberries have creeping runners that quickly and easily grow in burned or disturbed areas. Native Americans frequently burned fields and meadows to make walking and hunting easier. In 1776 botanist William Bartram traveled through western North Carolina fields, noting that his horse's legs were dyed red as he watched young Native Americans girls collecting abundant strawberries. Thomas Jefferson planted strawberries in his gardens. Useful and nutritious, the berries were made into jams, pies, and even wines. The yellow flowers of Indian or false strawberry (*Potentilla indica/Duchesnea indica*) (insets) are very similar in growth and habitat. Although edible, the red strawberry-like fruits lack flavor, and the dry inside is white rather than juicy red.

BOWMAN'S ROOT
Gillenia trifoliata
Rose family (Rosaceae)
Quick ID: White star-shaped flowers; 5 narrow, scraggly petals; alternate, nearly unstalked leaves divided into 3 narrow leaflets that are pointed and finely toothed; reddish stems thin and branching.
Height: 1'–3'   **Bloom Season:** May–July

The floppy petaled white flowers and weak stems of Bowman's root give this plant a relaxed, hassle-free appearance. Sometimes called American ipecac or mountain Indian physic, it was used as an emetic; the powdered root was administered until the patient vomited in an effort to cure the person's ailment. Bowman's root is one of the many plants noted by wildflower advocates Helen and Julia Smith. In the 1970s these two intrepid sisters rallied Parkway officials to reduce mowing operations along the roadway to spare the native wildflowers. A display of their photographs, catalogues, and observations can be seen at the Peaks of Otter Visitor Center. The genus name, *Gillenia*, honors Arnold Gill, a seventeenth-century German botanist and physician.

184

ALLEGHENY BLACKBERRY
Rubus alleghaniensis
Rose family (Rosaceae)
Quick ID: Arching angular stems with stout prickles; flowers with 5 white petals; leaves alternate, fan shaped with 3–7 serrated leaflets, pale below; gland-tipped hairs on branches; black berries.

Height: 3'–6'   **Bloom Season:** May–June

Mountain families living far from any sort of medical care had to rely on wild plants for many purposes, including food and medicine. Blackberries were widespread, and families along the Blue Ridge prized these prickly shrubs for their juicy, black berries, which were made into delightful pies and jams. Widely used as a treatment for diarrhea, a handful of blackberry roots were boiled and given to the sufferer as a tea. Wild cherry bark was sometimes added to this mixture. A thick syrup of blackberry tonic was kept on hand for tummy troubles. The leaves, shoots, roots, and berries were also used to dye cloth. The rambling stems bend over and root at the tips, often forming large thickets in open areas.

PARTRIDGEBERRY

Mitchella repens

Madder family (Rubiaceae)

Quick ID: Evergreen; 2 white ½" tubular flowers, 4 spreading lobes at end of stem, fuzzy inside; trailing woody stem; opposite, rounded leaves; hard, bright red berries.

Height: 4"–12" **Bloom Season:** May–July

Creeping along the ground, partridgeberry has rounded opposite leaves that are topped with 2 delightfully fuzzy white flowers that are joined at the base. White-tailed deer, raccoons, foxes, and birds eat the 1 bright-red berry that forms. American Indian women would drink a tea made from the berries and leaves of the plant 2 to 3 weeks before childbirth to ease labor pains. Nursing mothers also used an infusion of the plant for sore nipples. The tea was also used medicinally for menstrual cramps, diarrhea, and urinary difficulties. The tasteless berries could be eaten as a snack or made into a jelly. The genus name, *Mitchella*, honors Dr. John Mitchell (1711–1768), an early botanist from Virginia. The species name, *repens*, means "creeping."

AMERICAN LILY OF THE VALLEY
Convallaria pseudomajalis
Ruscus family (Ruscaceae)
Quick ID: White bell-shaped flowers hang from tiny stems on arching stem; 2–3 alternate, elliptic leaves 6"–12".
Height: 6"–11" **Bloom Season:** April–June

Growing in rich woods, 2 types of sweet-smelling lily of the valley can be found along the Blue Ridge Parkway. The introduced European lily of the valley (*C. majalis*) often forms dense colonies of flowers that spread by underground rhizomes. Large numbers of these flowers can often be found near old homesites, cemeteries, and roadsides. Not typically forming large colonies, it is found from Virginia to Georgia. American lily of the valley is endemic to the Southern Appalachians. After the flowers die away, the leaves remain into fall, when the orangey-red berries form. All parts of the plant are toxic, as it contains cardiac glycosides that cause heart arrhythmias. A large colony of European lily of the valley can be found at Whetstone Ridge.

CANADA MAYFLOWER
Maianthemum canadense
Ruscus family (Ruscaceae)
Quick ID: Evergreen; small white flowers on a single stem, 4 petals, 4 stamens; 2–3 smooth alternate leaves, pointed oval with a heart-shaped base that hugs the stem; green berries with red markings.
Height: 3¹⁄₁₀"–7⁹⁄₁₀"   **Bloom Season:** May–July

A widespread understory plant, Canada mayflower occurs in a variety of habitats, from valley forests to high-altitude meadows. As with most plants, the elevation level can greatly affect the blooming season. The small white flowers of Canada mayflower bloom in mid-May in the valleys but may not bloom until the end of June or early July at higher elevations. Canada mayflower is sometimes called false lily of the valley, as it somewhat resembles a small American lily of the valley (*Convallaria pseudomajalis*). The fruits that stay on the stems into spring provide food for birds such as grouse, which help spread the seeds away from the parent plant. Look for Canada mayflower along many trails in the park, including the Boone Fork and Mountains-to-Sea Trails.

ALLEGHENY BROOK SAXIFRAGE
Boykinia aconitifolia
Saxifrage family (Saxifragaceae)
Quick ID: White flowers on branching stems, 5 petals; sharply lobed maple-like leaves at the base and smaller leaves on the stem.
Height: 6"–35"　　　　　　　　　　　**Bloom Season:** June–July

If you want to see brook saxifrage, you often need to get your feet wet—it grows in seepage areas along streambanks and along rivers or waterfalls. You also have to come to the Southern Appalachians, as it grows nowhere else. It is sometimes mistaken for Carolina bugbane (*Trautvetteria caroliniensis*), but the bugbane's white flowers are not as delicate looking as those of Allegheny brook saxifrage. The genus, *Boykinia*, honors Dr. Samuel Boykin (1786–1848), a Georgia physician who discovered several species of plants. The leaves have sharp lobes that resemble those of monkshood (*Aconitum uncinatum*), hence the species name, *aconitifolia*. You can see Allegheny brook saxifrage blooming in the wet areas near Mabry Mill.

ROCK ALUMROOT
Heuchera villosa
Saxifrage family (Saxifragaceae)
Quick ID: Tiny white flowers on hairy stalk; maple-like basal leaves with 5–7 sharp lobes.
Height: 8"–36"   **Bloom Season:** June–October

The genus *Heuchera* has about 37 members in North America, and several species can be found in our area. Sometimes called maple-leaved or hairy alumroot, rock alumroot is commonly found in the Blue Ridge Mountains on high-elevation rock outcrops. The greenish-flowered common alumroot (*H. americana*) blooms earlier in spring. Native Americans used the roots of alumroot medicinally for dysentery, oral thrush, and bad sores. Plants contain small proteins called defensins, which keep the plant safe from fungal and some viral and bacterial attacks. Interestingly, oral thrush is caused by the candida fungus. Recent scientific studies have shown that this fungus is killed by the chemical components of alumroot.

MICHAUX'S CLIFF SAXIFRAGE
Hydatica petiolaris
Saxifrage family (Saxifragaceae)
Quick ID: Tiny white flowers on thin, wispy stems, 3 upper petals with 2 yellow spots, orange anthers; coarsely toothed spatula-shaped leaves.
Height: 4"–15"   **Bloom Season:** June–August

In the late 1700s, when there was little technical knowledge about the plant life of North America, a French botanist named André Michaux was one of the pioneers who explored much of the Appalachians. Many plants are named to honor him, including Michaux's cliff saxifrage. The family name, Saxifrage, means "stone breaker." The thin wispy stems of saxifrage are in no way strong enough to break rocks, but people once thought that they caused the cracks and crevices in the cliff faces and rock outcroppings where they bloom. Michaux's cliff saxifrage is one of the plants that has undergone taxonomic changes and in older references may be listed as *Micranthes petiolaris* or *Saxifraga michauxii*. Look for Michaux's cliff saxifrage growing along the cliffs at Waterrock Knob.

191

MITERWORT
Mitella diphylla
Saxifrage family (Saxifragaceae)
Quick ID: Tiny white ⅛" flowers on single stem, 5 fringed petals; 1 pair opposite, stalkless stem leaves that resemble small maple leaves.
Height: 10"–18"   **Bloom Season:** April–May

So delicate is this plant that it is often overlooked by passing hikers. This is unfortunate, as miterwort is one of nature's true masterpieces in miniature. Growing in moist areas, especially along streams, the tiny lace-trimmed, white flowers are best viewed with a magnifying glass; lacking that you can turn your binoculars backward to magnify the image. Magnified, the flowers look like tiny white snowflakes, prompting the common name snowflake flower. Wildflower photographers find this a particularly challenging plant to photograph—the slightest breeze sends these flowers moving. The genus name, *Mitella*, refers to the shape of the seed capsules, which resemble a tall, pointed, two-peaked Catholic bishop's hat called a miter, which led to another common name, bishop's cap.

APPALACHIAN GRASS OF PARNASSUS
Parnassia asarifolia
Grass of Parnassus family (Parnassiaceae)
Quick ID: White 1"–2" flower, 5 waxy petals with bright green veins; kidney-shaped leaf at base that appears to encircle the wiry stem.
Height: 8"–16"   **Bloom Season:** August–October

Appalachian grass of Parnassus is a striking wetland beauty found primarily at high-elevation bogs or a unique vertical cliff face bog such as Wolf Mountain Overlook at Milepost 424.8. Sometimes called kidney-leaf grass of Parnassus, this uncommon plant is not a grass at all, and it doesn't grow on Mount Parnassus in Greece. Grecian cattle did, however, enjoy grazing on a similar plant, hence the referral to grass. The 5 waxy white petals are etched with prominent green lines that guide insects to the nectaries at the base of
the petals. In the center of the dish-shaped flower are 5 stamens with grayish tips and conspicuous shorter structures called staminodes sporting bright yellow tips. Deeply cleft into 3 parts, staminodes are sterile stamens that do not produce pollen but aid in attracting pollinators.

LETTUCE LEAVED SAXIFRAGE
Micranthes micranthidifolia
Saxifrage family (Saxifragaceae)

Quick ID: White flowers on thin arching stems, 5 white, rounded petals with yellow dots at base; thin, sharply toothed, 12–40 teeth on each margin, lettuce-like leaves up to about 12".

Height: 12"–35"　　　　　　　　　　　　　**Bloom Season:** May–June

Shaded seepage areas along small streams are common in many areas along the Blue Ridge Parkway, and hikers may find small log bridges or stepping-stones to help traverse these areas. With its 2'-3' stems and small white flowers, lettuce leaved saxifrage is one of the most prominent plants seen in these shady areas. The plant is commonly called branch lettuce, referring to the term used for a small stream. Appalachian families enjoy a regional dish called "kilt" (killed) lettuce, or wilted lettuce, using the leaves of branch lettuce. After the leaves are gathered, hot bacon grease is poured over the leaves, causing them to wilt, or become "kilt." The tasty dish is often served with chopped spring onions from the garden, fried potatoes, and corn bread.

FOAMFLOWER
Tiarella cordifolia
Saxifrage family (Saxifragaceae)
Quick ID: Tiny white flowers clustered at end of leafless stem, 5 white petals often tinged pink, 10 yellowish-orange tipped stamens; heart-shaped leaves on stalk.
Height: 6"–12"   **Bloom Season:** April–June

The genus of wildflowers called *Tiarella* has only 5 total members, 2 from North America and 3 from Asia, some of which occur in the Himalayan Mountains. The connection between many North American plants and Asian plants is well documented, as many share a common ancestral species. Foamflower is one such plant, with *T. trifoliata* in western North America and *T. cordifolia* in the eastern states. Sometimes called heartleaf foamflower or false miterwort, foamflower grows in moist hollows and rich cove forests. The feathery white flowers somewhat resemble those of miterwort (*Mitella diphylla*) but lack the fringes. The soft, foam-like flowers are sometimes found in large colonies; look for foamflower along the trail to Crabtree Falls.

LARGE-FLOWERED TRILLIUM
Trillium grandiflorum
Trillium family (Trilliaceae)

Quick ID: Single white flower 2"–4" wide; 3 white oval petals with wavy edges turning pink with age flared toward pointed tip; 3 oval to diamond-shaped stalkless leaves.

Height: 8"–18" **Bloom Season:** April–May

Spring is heralded by many plants, but perhaps the most revered by wild-flower lovers is the large-flowered trillium. Honored as the representa-tive flower of Shenandoah National Park, trilliums are characterized by 3 petals, 3 sepals, and 3 leaves, hence the genus prefix *tri*, which means "three." Another white trillium found in the southern part of the Park-way is sweet white trillium (*T. simile*), which has broad white petals with nearly straight edges. While large-flowered trillium has little to no smell, sweet white trillium smells like green apples. Some trilliums have both a red form and a white form, such as red trillium (*T. erectum*). Unless you have a stuffy nose, the white morph of red trillium is easy to distin-guish—it smells like a wet dog.

SOUTHERN NODDING TRILLIUM

Trillium rugelii
Trillium family (Trilliaceae)
Quick ID: White or maroon flower on stalks that hangs below leaves, 3 recurved petals, purple anthers; 3 leaves in whorl.
Height: 6"–20"   **Bloom Season:** April–May

The petals of southern nodding trillium are normally white but can also be maroon. Found in the Southern Appalachians, the white or maroon flowers of this trillium hang below the leaves. The plant looks somewhat like Catesby's trillium (*T. catesbaei*), but the leaves are broader in southern nodding trillium. If you look closely at Catesby's trillium, you should notice the bright yellow anthers that have been described as "egg yolk" yellow. Southern nodding trillium is named to honor Ferdinand Rugel (1806–1879), a British botanist who collected plants in the Southern Appalachians in the mid-1800s.

197

PAINTED TRILLIUM
Trillium undulatum
Trillium family (Trilliaceae)

Quick ID: Single flower about 2" wide; white wavy-margined petals with reddish V-shaped markings in center; 3" oval, sharply pointed, stalked, coppery-green leaves with rounded base: fruit is red 3-angled berry.

Height: 8"–16"   **Bloom Season:** April–May

Of the 8 species of trillium that can be found along the Parkway, painted trillium is perhaps the easiest to identify to species. The 3 white petals are emblazoned with unique reddish V-shaped blazes at the base of each petal. The flower blossoms for about 3 weeks in April or May and is followed in fall by red berries with 3 angles. These trilliums prefer acidic soils, such as those typically found where acid-loving trees such as pines, spruce, and fir grow. Painted trilliums are found in the east from Canada to the high mountains of Georgia. Look for painted trillium on hikes through rich forests, such as the trail to Linville Falls or the Price Lake Loop Trail.

SWEET WHITE VIOLET
Viola blanda
Violet family (Violaceae)
Quick ID: White flowers, 5 petals with the upper 2 bent backward and twisted, lower petal has purple veins; reddish stalks coming from ground; heart-shaped shiny leaves that come to a point.
Height: 3"–5"   **Bloom Season:** April–May

Ranging in color from deep violet to yellow to white, more than 20 violet species can be found along the Blue Ridge Parkway. Sweet white violet is a "stemless" violet, meaning its stem arises directly from the ground rather than from other stems, with petals that reflex like a dog's ears. It also has yellow in the throat. Native Americans mixed the leaves and stems of violets including sweet white violet with other greens to be fried in fat and eaten. Primrose-leaf violet (*V. primulifolia*) has wedge-shaped leaves that taper at the base. Striped or creamy wood violet (*V. striata*) is a "stemmed" violet and the similar Canada violet (*V. canadensis*) has a yellow throat.

199

TURKEYBEARD
Xerophyllum asphodeloides
Beargrass family (Xerophyllaceae)

Quick ID: Small white flowers in dense, elongated, up to 12" long cluster atop thick stem; 1½'–2' long grasslike leaves in clump at base, tiny saw-like teeth on the edges; stem leaves bract-like.

Height: 2'–5'   **Bloom Season:** May–July

The tall white flowers of turkeybeard stand out like white torches on mountain meadows along the Blue Ridge Parkway. The up to 2' long grasslike leaves form a clump at the base of the plant. Only 1 other species shares the genus *Xerophyllum* with turkeybeard, but the very similar common beargrass (*X. tenax*) is only found in western North America. Turkeybeard grows in two disjunct locations: here in the Southern Appalachians and also in the pine barrens of New Jersey. Due to special adaptations, large displays of turkeybeard can occur after a fire. Fly poison (*Amianthium muscaetoxicum*) has similar flowers, but its leaves are wider. Nearby Grandfather Mountain is a great place to see turkeybeard, near the swinging bridge area.

Glossary

Alkaloid—bitter compounds produced by plants to discourage predators.

Alternate leaves—growing singly on a stem without an opposite leaf.

Anther—tip of a flower's stamen that produces pollen grains.

Bald—primarily found on Southern Appalachian mountain summits or crests, balds are areas covered by heath shrubs or grasses and generally lack trees.

Basal—at the base or bottom.

Bulb—underground structure made up of layered, fleshy scales.

Capsule—a dry fruit that releases seeds through splits or holes.

Compound leaf—a leaf that is divided into two or more leaflets.

Corm—rounded, solid underground stem.

Deciduous—a plant that seasonally loses its leaves.

Detritus—leaf litter and decaying wood and other organic material mixed with soil.

Doctrine of Signatures—a seventeenth-century belief that plants display a sign that indicates its medicinal use.

Ecosystem—a biological environment consisting of all the living organisms in a particular area as well as the nonliving components, such as water, soil, air, and sunlight.

Endemic—growing only in a specific region or habitat.

Escaped—a plant that grows and reproduces where it was not originally planted.

Ethnobotany—the study of the relationship between plants and people.

Evergreen—a tree that keeps its leaves (often needles) year-round.

Genus—taxonomic rank below family and above species; always capitalized and italicized.

Habitat—the area or environment where an organism lives or occurs.

Introduced—a species living outside its native range; often introduced by human activity.

Leaflet—a part of a compound leaf; may resemble an entire leaf but is borne on a vein of a leaf rather than the stem. Leaflets are referred to as pinnae; the compound leaves are pinnate (featherlike).

Lobe—a rounded projection.

Native—a species indigenous or endemic to an area.

Nectar—sweet liquid produced by flowers to attract pollinators.

Nectary—a nectar-secreting structure on a leaf or stem of a flower.

Niche—an organism's response to available resources and competitors (like a human's job).

Nocturnal—active at night.

Opposite leaves—growing in pairs along the stem.

Ovary—the enlarged base of the female reproductive structure of a flower (pistil) where the ovules (undeveloped seeds) are produced.

Palmate—three or more lobes that are shaped like an outstretched palm.

Parasitism—one organism benefits at the expense of another organism.

Perfoliate—leaves are united at the base and appear to be pierced by the stem.

Pinnate—divided or lobed along each side of a leaf stalk, resembling a feather.

Pistil—the ovule (undeveloped seed) producing part of a flower made up of the stigma, style, and ovary.

Pollen—small powdery particles that contain the plant's male sex cells.

Pollination—transfer of pollen from an anther (male) to a stigma (female).

Rachis—main axis or shaft; in plants the main stem of a flower cluster or compound leaf.

Rhizome—underground stem that grows horizontally and sends up shoots.

Riparian—area between land and a stream or river.

Sepal—usually green leaflike structures found underneath the flower.

Serrated—having a jagged or zigzag edge on a leaf with continuous, sharp teeth that point forward.

Simple leaf—a leaf that is not divided into parts.

Sinus—indentations between lobes on a leaf.

Species—taxonomic rank below genus; always italicized but never capitalized; also called "specific epithet."

Spine—modified leaves or stipules that form sharp projections.

Stamen—male part of the flower; composed of a filament, or stalk, and anther, the sac at the tip of the filament that produces pollen.

Staminode—rudimentary, sterile stamen that does not produce pollen.

Stigma—the part of the female reproductive part of a plant (pistil) where the pollen germinates.

Style—the part of the female reproductive part of a plant (pistil) structure that connects the stigma to the ovary.

Symbiosis—association of unlike organisms that benefits one or both.

Taxonomy—study of scientific classifications.

Tepal—indistinguishable petals and sepals.

Thorn—a modified branch or stem that forms a sharp woody projection.

Toothed—jagged or serrated edge, not necessarily pointed.

Tuber—underground thickened part of stem or rhizome that serves as a nutrient reserve.

Umbel—several to many short flower stalks that spread from a common point.

Whorl—a ring of three or more parts radiating from one point.

Winged—thin, flattened expansion on the sides of a plant part.

Selected References

Abramson, R., and J. Haskell, eds. *Encyclopedia of Appalachia*. Knoxville, TN: University of Tennessee Press, 2006.

Adams, K. *North Carolina's Best Wildflower Hikes: The Mountains*. Englewood, CO: Westcliffe Publishers, Inc., 2004.

Adkins, L. M. *Hiking and Traveling the Blue Ridge Parkway*. Chapel Hill, NC: University of North Carolina Press, 2013.

———. *Walking the Blue Ridge*, third edition. Chapel Hill, NC: The University of North Carolina Press, 2006.

———. *Wildflowers of the Blue Ridge and Great Smoky Mountains*. Birmingham, AL: Menasha Ridge Press, 2005.

Alderman, J. A. *Wildflowers of the Blue Ridge Parkway*. Chapel Hill, NC: The University of North Carolina Press, 1997.

Amjad, H. *Folk Medicine of Appalachia*. LaVergne, TN: Lulu Press, 2006.

Banks, W. H. *Ethnobotany of the Cherokee Indians*. Master's thesis, University of Tennessee, 1953; trace.tennessee.edu/utk_gradthes/1052.

———. *Plants of the Cherokee*. Gatlinburg, NC: Great Smoky Mountains Association, 2004.

Bell, R. B., and A. H. Lindsey. *Fall Color and Woodland Harvests*. Chapel Hill, NC: Laurel Hill Press, 1990.

Bentley, S. L. *Native Orchids of the Southern Appalachian Mountains*. Chapel Hill, NC: The University of North Carolina Press, 2000.

Bolgiano, C. *The Appalachian Forest: A Search for Roots and Renewal*. Mechanicsburg, PA: Stackpole Books, 1998.

Bolyard, J. L. *Medicinal Plants and Home Remedies of Appalachia*. Springfield, IL: Charles C. Thomas Publisher, 1981.

Brooks, M. *The Appalachians*. Boston, MA: Houghton Mifflin Company, 1965.

Catlin, D. T. *A Naturalist's Blue Ridge Parkway*. Knoxville, TN: The University of Tennessee Press, 1984.

Cavender, A. *Folk Medicine in Southern Appalachia*. Chapel Hill, NC: The University of North Carolina Press, 2003.

Church, B. *Medicinal Plants, Trees & Shrubs of Appalachia*, second edition. Mustang, OK: Tate Publishing & Enterprises, LLC, 2012.

Clemants, S., and C. Gracie. *Wildflowers in the Field and Forest: A Field Guide to the Northeastern United States.* New York, NY: Oxford University Press, Inc., 2006.

Constantz, G. *Hollows, Peepers & Highlanders*, second edition. Morgantown, WV: West Virginia University Press, 2004.

Davis, J. P. *Five-Star Trails: Asheville.* Birmingham, AL: Menasha Ridge Press, 2012.

Duncan, W. H., and M. B. Duncan. *Wildflowers of the Eastern United States.* Athens, GA: The University of Georgia Press, 1999.

Elliott, D. *Wild Roots.* Rochester, VT: Healing Arts Press, 1995.

Erichsen-Brown, C. *Medicinal and Other Uses of North American Plants.* New York, NY: Dover Publications, Inc., 1979.

Fisher, E. *Thrilling Trilies & Captivating Cattails.* Staunton, VA: Lot's Wife Publishing, 2006.

Frick-Ruppert, J. *Mountain Nature: A Seasonal Natural History of the Southern Appalachians.* Chapel Hill, NC: The University of North Carolina Press, 2010.

Gaddy, L. L. *Alpine South Plants and Plant Communities of the High Elevations of the Southern Appalachians.* Terra Incognita Books, 2014; www.tibooks.org.

Garrett, J. T. *The Cherokee Herbal.* Rochester, VT: Bear & Company, 2003.

Gunn, J. C., and J. H. Jordan. *Gunn's New Domestic Physician*, or *Home Book of Health: A Complete Guide for Families.* Cincinnati, OH: Moore, Wilstach, Keys & Company, 1861.

Hall, K. C. *Ethnobotany of the Eastern Band of the Cherokee Indians.* Charleston, SC: Emerald Wing Press LLC, 2010.

Harris, M. *Botanica North America.* New York, NY: HarperCollins Publishers, Inc., 2003.

Hemmerly, T. E. *Appalachian Wildflowers.* Athens, GA: The University of Georgia Press, 2000.

Horn, D., and R. Cathcart. *Wildflowers of Tennessee, the Ohio Valley, and the Southern Appalachians.* Auburn, WA: Lone Pine Publishing and the Tennessee Native Plant Society, 2005.

Howell, P. K. *Medicinal Plants of the Southern Appalachians.* Mountain City, GA: BotanoLogos Books, 2006.

Hutchens, A. R. *A Handbook of Native American Herbs.* Boston, MA: Shambhala Publications, Inc., 1992.

Integrated Taxonomic Information System (ITIS); itis.gov.

Jeffries, S. B., and T. R. Wentworth. *Exploring Southern Appalachian Forests.* Chapel Hill, NC: The University of North Carolina Press, 2014.

Johnson, R. *Best Easy Day Hikes Blue Ridge Parkway*, second edition. Guilford, CT: Globe Pequot Press / FalconGuides, 2010.

———. *Hiking the Blue Ridge Parkway*, 2nd ed. Guilford, CT: Globe Pequot Press / FalconGuides, 2010.

Joslin, M. *Appalachian Bounty.* Johnson City, TN: The Overmountain Press, 2000.

Justice, W. S., C. R. Bell, and A. H. Lindsey. *Wild Flowers of North Carolina*, second edition. Chapel Hill, NC: The University of North Carolina Press, 2005.

Kirkland, J., H. F. Mathews, C. W. Sullivan and K. Baldwin, eds. *Herbal and Magical Medicine: Traditional Healing Today.* Durham, NC: Duke University Press, 1992.

Krochmal, A., R. S. Walters, and R. M. Doughty. *A Guide to Medicinal Plants of Appalachia.* Honolulu, HI: University Press of the Pacific, 2005.

Logue, V., F. Logue, and N. Blouin. *Guide to the Blue Ridge Parkway*, third edition. Birmingham, AL: Menasha Ridge Press, 2010.

Lord, W. G. *Blue Ridge Parkway Guide: Rockfish Gap to Grandfather Mountain 0.0 to 291.9 Miles.* Birmingham, AL: Menasha Ridge Press, 1981.

———. *Blue Ridge Parkway Guide: Grandfather Mountain to Great Smoky Mountain National Park 291.9 to 469 Miles.* Birmingham, AL: Menasha Ridge Press, 1981.

Medina, B., and V. Medina. *Central Appalachian Wildflowers.* Guilford, CT: Globe Pequot Press / FalconGuides, 2002.

———. *Southern Appalachian Wildflowers.* Guilford, CT: Globe Pequot Press / FalconGuides, 2002.

Meuninck, J. *Medicinal Plants of North America.* Guilford, CT: Globe Pequot Press / FalconGuides, 2008.

Meyer, J. E. *The Old Herb Doctor*, second edition. Fairview, NC: Bright Mountain Books, Inc. 2009.

Midgley, J. W. *Southeastern Wildflowers.* Birmingham, AL: Crane Hill Publishers, 1999.

Miller, J. H., and K. V. Miller. *Forest Plants of the Southeast and Their Wildlife Uses*, revised edition. Athens, GA: University of Georgia Press, 2005.

Moerman, D. E. *Native American Ethnobotany.* Portland, ME: Timber Press, Inc., 1998.

————. *Native American Ethnobotany: A Database of Foods, Drugs, Dyes and Fibers of Native American Peoples, Derived from Plants.* Dearborn, MI: University of Michigan; herb.umd.umich.edu.

Moss, K. K. *Southern Folk Medicine 1750–1820.* Columbia, SC: University of South Carolina Press, 1999.

Peterson, R. T., and M. McKenny. *A Field Guide to Wildflowers: Wildflowers Northeastern and North Central North America.* Boston, MA: Houghton Mifflin Company, 1968.

Petrides, G. A. *A Field Guide to Trees and Shrubs*, second edition. New York, NY: Houghton Mifflin Company, 1986.

Porcher, F. P. *Resources of the Southern Fields and Forests, Medical, Economical, and Agricultural. Being also a Medical Botany of the Confederate States; with Practical Information on the Useful Properties of the Trees, Plants, and Shrubs; 1863.* Chapel Hill, NC: University of North Carolina. Electronic edition, 2000.

Radford, A. E., H. E. Ahles, and C. R. Bell. *Manual of the Vascular Flora of the Carolinas.* Chapel Hill, NC: The University of North Carolina Press, 1968.

Saunders, J. *The Secrets of Wildflowers.* Guilford, CT: Globe Pequot Press, 2003.

Simmons, N. *Best of the Blue Ridge Parkway.* Johnson City, TN: Mountain Trail Press, 2008.

Simpson, A., and R. Simpson. *Nature Guide to the Blue Ridge Parkway.* Guilford, CT: Morris Book Publishing, LLC, 2013.

————. *Wildflowers of Shenandoah National Park.* Guilford, CT: Morris Book Publishing, LLC, 2011.

Smith, R. M. *Wildflowers of the Southern Mountains.* Knoxville, TN: The University of Tennessee Press, 1998.

Spira, T. P. *Waterfalls & Wildflowers in the Southern Appalachians.* Chapel Hill, NC: The University of North Carolina Press, 2015.

————. *Wildflowers & Plant Communities of the Southern Appalachian Mountains & Piedmont.* Chapel Hill, NC: The University of North Carolina Press, 2011.

Stokes, D. W. *The Natural History of Wild Shrubs and Vines.* New York, NY: Harper & Row, 1981.

Sumner, J. *The Natural History of Medicinal Plants.* Portland, OR: Timber Press, 2000.

Tennessee Flora Committee, eds. *Guide to the Vascular Plants of Tennessee.* Knoxville, TN: The University of Tennessee Press, 2015.

Thieret, J. W., W. A. Niering, and N. C. Olmstead. *National Audubon Society Field Guide to North American Wildflowers Eastern Region*, revised edition. New York, NY: Alfred A. Knopf, Inc. / Chanticleer Press, Inc., 2001.

Virginia Botanical Associates. Digital Atlas of the Virginia Flora (vaplantatlas .org) (c/o Virginia Botanical Associates, Blacksburg, VA, 2016).

Weakley, A. S. *Flora of the Southern and Mid-Atlantic States*, May 2015 version. UNC Herbarium, North Carolina Botanical Garden, University of North Carolina at Chapel Hill; herbarium.unc.edu/flora.htm.

Weakley, A. S., J. C. Ludwig, and J. F. Townsend. *Flora of Virginia*. Fort Worth, TX: Botanical Research Institute of Texas Press, 2012.

Wells, D. *100 Flowers and How They Got Their Names*. New York, NY: Algonquin Books of Chapel Hill / Workman Publishing, 1997.

Wigginton, E., and his students, eds. *Foxfire 3*. New York, NY: Anchor Books / Random House, Inc., 1975.

Index

216

About the Authors

Professional photographers, biologists, authors, and noted national park experts, Ann and Rob Simpson have spent years involved with research and interpretation in US national parks. They have written numerous books on national parks coast to coast that promote conservation and proper use of natural habitats and environmental stewardship. As a former chief of interpretation and national park board member, Rob has a unique understanding of the inner workings of the National Park System. In cooperation with American Park Network, both have led Canon "Photography in the Parks" workshops in major national parks including Yosemite, Yellowstone, Grand Canyon, and Great Smoky Mountains.

Ann and Rob are both award-winning biology professors at Lord Fairfax Community College in Middletown, Virginia. With a background in science education, Ann heads the science department. As part of the college's Nature Photography curriculum, the Simpsons regularly lead international photo tours to parks and natural history destinations around the world.

Long known for their stunning images of the natural world, their work has been widely published in such magazines as *National Geographic, Time, National Wildlife*, and *Ranger Rick*, as well as many calendars, postcards, and books. Both are members of the Virginia Outdoor Writers Association, Mason Dixon Outdoor Writers Association, and Outdoor Writers Association of America. You can see their work at Simpson's Nature Photography: annrobsimpson.com.